PEGASUS DESCENDING

PEGASUS DESCENDING

A Book of the Best Bad Verse

edited with notes and an introductory dialogue
by James Camp, X. J. Kennedy
and Keith Waldrop

"To have great poets there must
be great audiences too."
—Walt Whitman

BURNING DECK, PROVIDENCE

Burning Deck
71 Elmgrove Ave., Providence RI 02906
Burning Deck is the literature program of Anyart: Contemporary Arts Center, a tax-exempt (501c3), non-profit organization.

Library of Congress Catalog Card Number: 79-144150
ISBN 1-886224-68-4

First printed by The Macmillan Company (Collier Books).

Cover by Keith Waldrop

ACKNOWLEDGMENTS

Illustrations by Paul Flora from the book *Das Musenross* are reproduced here by arrangement with the publisher Diogenes Verlag Zurich © 1955 by Daniel Keel/Diogenes Verlag.

For arrangements made with authors, their representatives, and publishing houses who permitted the use of copyrighted material, the following acknowledgments are gratefully made. All possible care has been taken to trace the ownership of selections included. If any errors have accidentally occurred, they will be corrected in subsequent editions, provided notice is sent to the editors in care of the publisher.

Burns & Oates Ltd., for the poem "The Shepherdess" by Alice Meynell, reprinted by permission of Messrs. Burns & Oates Ltd. and the Executors of the estate of Mrs. Alice Meynell.

Dr. A. Rasheed Ghazi for "A Poem on the I.U.D.," reprinted by permission of the author.

G. P. Putnam's Sons for passages from "The Indictment" by F. F. Ayer, from *Bell and Wing* by Frederick Fanning Ayer (New York: G. P. Putnam's Sons, 1911). Reprinted by permission of the publisher.

Henry Regnery Company for the quotation from "The Crucible of Life" by Edgar A. Guest, from *Just Folks* by Edgar A. Guest (Chicago: Reilly & Lee Company, 1915). Reprinted by permission of Henry Regnery Company.

Charles Scribner's Sons for the quotation from "The House on the Hill" by Edwin Arlington Robinson, from *The Children of the Night* by Edwin Arlington Robinson (New York: Charles Scribner's Sons, 1897); and for "The Shepherdess" by Alice Meynell, from *The Poems of Alice Meynell* (New York: Charles Scribner's Sons, 1893). Reprinted by permission of the publisher.

Thacker & Company Ltd., for the poem "Shirley Temple" by C. R. Michael, from *Come Back to Hindustan and Me* by Cyril R. Michael (Bombay, India: Thacker & Company Ltd., 1941). Reprinted by permission of the publisher.

Ali Sedat Hilmi Torël for selections from *Verse at Random* by Ali S. Hilmi (Larnaca, Cyprus: Ohanian Press, 1953). Reprinted by permission of the author.

Harvard University Press for the poems by Emily Dickinson "He was weak, and I was strong" and "A Dying Tiger Moaned for Drink" and quotations from the poems by Emily Dickinson "Dying at my music" and "Our lives are Swiss." Reprinted by permission of the publishers and the Trustees of Amherst College from Thomas H. Johnson, editor, *The Poems of Emily Dickinson* (Cambridge, Mass.: The Belknap Press of Harvard University Press). Copyright 1951, 1955 by the President and Fellows of Harvard College.

The Macmillan Company for quotations from the following poems in *Collected Poems* by Thomas Hardy: "Nothing Matters Much," reprinted with permission of The Macmillan Company; copyright 1925 by The Macmillan Company, renewed 1953 by Lloyds Bank Ltd.; "That Kiss in the Dark,' reprinted with permission of The Macmillan Company; copyright 1928 by Florence E. Hardy and Sydney E. Cockerell, renewed 1956 by Lloyds Bank Ltd.; "The Abbey Mason," "The Beauty," "The Convergence of the Twain," and "A Jog-trot Pair," reprinted with permission of The Macmillan Company; copyright 1925 by The Macmillan Company. Reprinted also with permission of the Trustees of the Estate of Thomas Hardy and with permission of Macmillan & Co. Ltd., London, and The Macmillan Company of Canada Ltd.

Charles E. Tuttle Co., Inc., for the poem "The Spirit's Odyssey" ("I saw her first in gleams") and for quotations from "The Cloth of Gold" by M. Krishnamurti, from *The Cloth of Gold: Poems* by M. Krishnamurti (Rutland, Vermont: Charles E. Tuttle Co., Inc.). Reprinted by permission of the publisher.

Contents

Epistle Dedicatory

TO C. M.

Great Carl! who stuck our noses to a scent
And set us raking heaps of excrement,
You New York editors play musical chairs
As hedgehogs quit their late-befoulèd lairs.
Yet you it was who swung the legs of us
Three on the broad beam of our Pegasus;
Or rather, lured us to come dabble snout
In that which some before us had let out.
Anthologies, they say, may not be dedicated;
Anthologists may be, though. What rimes here?
Medicated?)
Thus, should our Pegasus reek of pure horse,
Partake, O Carl, in this our pure re-Morse.

TO THE SINCERE READER:

Some poets in this book have roosted in more than one pigeonhole. On a poet's first entrance, a critical, biographical, or merely snide note has been provided. Except where vital for explanation, such notes are dispensed with on his later reappearances.

The editors owe much to friends and admirers on whose advice or inspiration they have leaned heavily. Among these are Dainis Bisenieks, Virginia Chamberlain, Martin B. Friedman, Hayden Goldberg, Joseph Reed, Mark Spilka, Paul G. Stanwood, Barton St. Armand, Ann Watts, Dallas Wiebe, Galen Williams, and John Barton Wolgamot. From William Cole, whose own *Fireside Book of Humorous Poetry* (New York, 1959) includes some bad verse, we received copies of several gems; and from Richard Walser, whose *Nematodes in My Garden of Verse* (Winston-Salem, 1959) does the job for the state of North Carolina, we have pilfered shamelessly. With all who labor in this vineyard, we early contracted a debt to that classic anthology, *The Stuffed Owl*, of D. B. Wyndham Lewis and Charles Lee (London, 1930). Except for two or three items given in full or more fully, we have strived not to duplicate its contents, but to keep its faith. More thanks than tongue can tell belong to Jocelyn A. Camp, Dorothy M. Kennedy, and Rosmarie S. Waldrop —who labored and endured.

A letter to Exposition Press, asking permission to reprint lines from one of their authors, and pointing out that it would seem no shame to keep company with such immortals as Keats and Tennyson, was returned with the superscription, "*Who are you kidding?*"

The publishers of Robert Frost couldn't see our including "A Girl's Garden," but the curious may find it in Frost's *Collected Poems*.

J.C.
X.J.K.
K.W.

PREFATORY DIALOGUE

(*Three learned friends, drifting down the East River in a vast pigskin canoe, discuss with zeal the name and nature of bad verse, after the fashion of the participants in Dryden's* Essay of Dramatic Poesy. *In the conversation that follows, the name* Pedanticus *will represent Mr. Keith Waldrop; the name* Ubuquitous, *Mr. James Camp; and the name* Coprophilius, *Mr. Xerox J. Kennedy.*)

Sound effects: Booming cannon of the Dutch, trying to retake New York.

Ubuquitous: God! the river's clean today.

Pedanticus: What is bad poetry?

Coprophilius: To answer that, Pedanticus, must we not ascertain the nature of Poetry herself; and, having done so, refresh us in the wisdom of Saint Thomas that badness does not exist as a positive quality, but may be beheld only in the absence of the good?

Ubuquitous: Haven't seen a banana peel for hours.

Pedanticus: How, now, Coprophilius, you confront us with an impossibility from the start. None but a fool would undertake to define the nature of Poetry. Let us be tentative: is not good bad verse a kind of performance in which there appears a ludicrous gap between whatever the writer has set himself to achieve, and the level of his talent and intelligence? Look, jeez, I mean, it's like seeing a guy get up on a diving tower and pose for a swan dive, and then he does a belly-whopper.

Coprophilius: You imply, then, an element of chance?

Pedanticus: At least, an element of the unintentional. In poetry, sincere failures are the only delectable kind. Whatever is consciously, deliberately bad—that must be shunned like some loathsome beetle or moral leper. Hence, the lines on an expiring frog that Dickens in *Pickwick Papers* casts into the mouth of a poetess—rotten as they are—can hold small joy for lovers of the true poetic awful. Hence, the brilliant lines that John Frederick Nims has blamed upon the fictitious bad poet Joe E. Skilmer:

Time is a toadstool on the nose of love . . .

and:

Once more at dawn I drive
The weary cattle of my soul to the mudhole of your eyes . . .

stand in relation to sincere bad verse somewhat as a good cigar to a wooden Indian.

Ubuquitous: There goes one now.

Pedanticus: One what?

Coprophilius: But do you imply, Pedanticus, that all bad verse is the product of simple minds, misled by an excess of devotion, into dilemmas beyond their capacities? Not so, not so. How often it is that bad verse is needlessly complicated! Such is the work of the bard who beats us over the heads with a brilliant display of excessive ingenuity; who has to be tricksy at all costs when (instead) he ought to be passionate. He it is who must lard his lines with alliteration just for the hell of it; who, called on for a paean, delivers a pun. His is the irresistible temptation that beset Poe, who in "For Annie" has a corpse remark that it feels "better at length." I would qualify your view of simple-mindedness, you simple-minded . . .

Pedanticus: Who said anything about simple-mindedness?

Coprophilius (*warming to his soliloquy*):

Yet I concur that good bad verse touches us upon

our most tender buttons, pains our most sensitive nerve centers! Randall Jarrell, you recall, says in *Poetry and the Age* that a bad poem comes on as though the writer were offering one of his severed members, scrawled with the lipstick motto, "This is a poem." Is this not true of that anonymous plea once addressed to Julius and Ethel Rosenberg as they awaited the electric chair, "Oh, be not fried!"? We respond to such a line, as we respond to all profound comedy: it would hurt not to laugh.

Pedanticus: Next you're going to pull Freud on us.

Coprophilius: Never! As Freud failed to observe, true bad verse may be the prerogative of the greatest bards. Mediocre poets seldom fail, they do but keep the great grey tenor of their ways. What think you. Ubuquitous?

Ubuquitous: (*Deep breathing.*)

Pedanticus: He's asleep.

Coprophilius: Why, too, is the most enormous bad verse usually rimed and metrical? How is it that so little bad free verse is funny?

Pedanticus: Good bad verse is like cheese, it must age before it be edible.

Coprophilius: And most free verse hasn't been around long enough? True, perhaps, but let me stick my neck out. In free verse, as in any other sort of poetry, a writer cannot long be fugg-headed, lazy, or incompetent without the reader's catching wise to him; but surely an inept free-versifier can escape detection longer than an incompetent sonneteer. If, with D. H. Lawrence, the poet views his work as a kind of spontaneous declamation, no one will laugh if his free verse contains a few natural stutters and imperfections. But writing a formal ode, on the other hand, is like singing an aria: a dangerous thing to belch in the middle of.

Pedanticus (*who all the while has been scribbling an immense free verse epic*):

Aaaaa, Coprophilius, you're full of it as a Christmas goose.

Ubuquitous (*in his sleep*):

Eureka! It all coheres! The essential nature of bad poetry may be defined . . .

Sound effects: Eight minutes of ear-splitting tugboat whistles.

Pedanticus: Bravo! Brilliant!

Coprophilius: You have solved, Ubuquitous, the whole vexing question. Let us now to the bookseller with our anthology, but if readers it should find, let them be warned not to read the entire book at a sitting.

Pedanticus: There used to be a beer, made in Michigan, of which it was said that the more of it one drank, the more he was made sober. So may it be with good bad verse. The prudent will indeed beware of mornings-after.

Invocation

Teach me to sing, O Muse, or rather neigh—
Nay, soar! And with what gall and hard travail
Ride thy fleet pasterns (down,
Sam Johnson, down—down, down, I say!)
And tufted pinions up, up and away!—
Not heeding Boanerges' wail
Nor with Bacchus, nor with starry Fay,
But with downward measured count
Mounting the Apollonian mount,
Blast off beyond Aonia to where
Pegasus can descend to stamp
His hooves upon some rugged lunar mare
And with his eager penetration there
Justify to man the ways of

—Camp

I

Openers

(a little treasury of worst opening lines)

. . . Virtuous youth!
Thank Heaven, I knew thee not!

—Christopher Ansty, Esq., "On the Much Lamented Death of the Marquis of Tavistock"

Creep into thy narrow bed,
Creep, and let no more be said!

—Matthew Arnold, "The Last Word"

Who prop, thou ask'st, in these bad days, my mind?

—Matthew Arnold, "To a Friend"

Fear not, grand eagle,
The bay of the beagle!

—Fred Emerson Brooks, "Old Eagle"

My love is not a soldier bold,
Because there is no war.

—Fred Emerson Brooks, "I Love My Love"

To live within a cave—it is most good.

—T. E. Brown, "Salve!"

We saw her die, and she is dead—

—T. E. Brown, "Symphony"

Morning, evening, noon, and night,
"Praise God!" said Theocrite.

—Robert Browning, "The Boy and the Angel"

"Summer is coming, summer is coming.
  I know it, I know it, I know it.
Light again, leaf again, life again, love again!"
  Yes, my wild little Poet.

—Robert Browning, "The Throstle"

Dear Mother,
                When the coach rolled off
  From dear old Battery Place,
I hid my face within my hands—
  That is, I hid my face.

—H. C. Bunner, "Their Wedding Journey—1834"

Sir, upon casting an attentive look
Over your friend, the learned Sherlock's, book,

One thing occurs about the FALL OF MAN
That does not suit with the Mosaic plan . . .

—John Byrom, "An Epistle to a Gentleman of the Temple, occasioned by Two Treatises, wherein the Fall of Man is differently represented, viz. I. Mr. Law's Spirit of Prayer. II. The Bishop of London's Appendix, Showing that, according to the plainest sense of Scripture, the Nature of the Fall is greatly mistaken in the latter"

Lauder! thy authors Dutch and German
There is no need to disinter, man!

—John Byrom, "Verses Intended to have been spoken at the commencement of the vacation of the Free Grammar School in Manchester, in the year 1748"

Standing on tiptoe ever since my youth . . .

—George Frederick Cameron, "Standing on Tiptoe"

Mother of God! no lady thou . . .

—Mary Elizabeth Coleridge, untitled poem

I'm back again! I'm back again!

—Eliza Cook, "My Native Home"

The Name of BELCHER long has Bless'd the State . . .

—John Danforth, "An Elegy Upon the Much Lamented Decease of the Reverend and Excellent Mr. Joseph Belcher"

Dying at my music!
Bubble! Bubble!

—Emily Dickinson, untitled poem

Our lives are Swiss—
So still—so Cool—

—Emily Dickinson, untitled poem

Can I see thee stand
On the looming land?

—Sydney Dobell, "Farewell"

She is gamesome and good,
But of mutable mood . . .

—Ralph Waldo Emerson, "Nature (ii)"

Fie, Aphrodite, shamming you are no mother,
And your maternal markings trying to smother . . .

—Thomas Hardy, "The Bad Example"

"Nothing matters much," he said
Of something just fallen unduly:
He, then active, but now dead,
  Truly, truly.

—Thomas Hardy, "Nothing Matters Much"

Recall it you?—
Say you do!—

—Thomas Hardy, "That Kiss in the Dark"

The Eurydice—it concerned thee, O Lord:
Three hundred souls, O alas! on board . . .

—Gerald Manley Hopkins, "The Loss of the Eurydice"

Methinks it is good to be here.

—Herbert Knowles, "The Three Tabernacles: Lines Written in the Churchyard of Richmond, Yorkshire"

As Gertrude skipped from babe to girl,
Her necklace lengthened, pearl by pearl . . .

—Frederick Locker-Lampson, "Gertrude's Necklace"

You ask a Song,
Such as of yore, an autumn's eventide,
Some blest Boy-Poet caroll'd,—and then died.
Nay, *I* have sung too long.

—Frederick Locker-Lampson, "My Song"

Kulnasatz, my reindeer,
We have a long journey to go!

—Lapland song, translator anonymous

The Gods on thrones celestial seated,
By Jove with bowls of nectar heated,
All on Mount Edgecumbe turn'd their eyes . . .

—George Lyttleton, "Mount Edgecumbe"

I kiss you, dear, and very sweet is this,
To feel you are not tainted by my kiss.

—Philip Bourke Marston, "To a Child"

Sleep, my little papoose;
Thy father hunteth the moose.
—Harry Edward Mills, "The Squaw's Lullaby"

Down south the Libby prison stood,
The rebel's filthy den;
Rebs in battle took—
Of course our Union men.
—Julia A. Moore, "Libby Prison"

Andrew was a little infant,
And his life was two years old . . .
—Julia A. Moore, "Little Andrew"

Little Charlie Hades has gone
To dwell with God above . . .
—Julia A. Moore, "Little Charlie Hades"

Some enterprising people,
In our cities and towns,
Have gone to organizing clubs
Of men that's fallen down.
—Julia A. Moore, "Temperance Reform Clubs"

Why does azure deck the sky?
'Tis to be like thy looks of blue . . .
—Thomas Moore, "Song"

Put off the vestal veil, nor, oh!—
Let weeping angels view it!
—Thomas Moore, "To ———, On Seeing Her With a White Veil and a Rich Girdle"

There are who, bending supple knees,
  Live for no end except to please,
Rising to fame by mean degrees;
  But creep not thou with these.

—Sir Lewis Morris, "Courage!"

The bowers whereat, in dreams, I see
  The wantonest singing birds,
Are lips—

—Edgar Allan Poe, "To ———"

I saw thee once—once only—years ago!
I must not say *how* many—but *not* many.

—Edgar Allan Poe, "To Helen"

Sweet Dog! now cold and stiff in death,
What cruel hand enticed thee here?
Did toothsome crust or juicy bone
Allure to stretch thee on thy bier?

—Georgia Bailey Purrington, "An Elegy to a Dissected Puppy"

'Ras Wilson, I respect you, 'cause
You're common, like you allus was . . .

—James Whitcomb Riley, "Erasmus Wilson"

They are all gone away,
  The House is shut and still,
There is nothing more to say.

—Edwin Arlington Robinson, "The House on the Hill"

O Health! capricious maid!

—William Shenstone, "Ode to Health"

Miranda! mark where shrinking from the gale,
  Its silken leaves yet moist with early dew,
That fair faint flower, the Lily of the vale
  Droops its meek head, and looks, methinks, like
    you!

—Charlotte Smith, "To an Amiable Girl"

Princely offspring of Braganza,
Erin greets thee with a stanza . . .

—Stott, "Ode" (on the departure of the reigning family from Portugal; quoted by Byron in the notes to *English Bards, and Scotch Reviewers*)

Thy mind was masculine—a sunbeam bright—

—Emma Tatham, "To Hannah More"

I love the dead!

—Martin Tupper, "The Dead. A Dirge."

In the prison cell we sit—
Are we broken-hearted?—Nit!

—William Whalen, "The Prison Song" (from *I.W.W. Songs to Fan the Flames of Discontent*)

I was asking for something specific and perfect for
    my city,
Whereupon lo! upsprang the aboriginal name.

—Walt Whitman, "Mannahatta"

Unfolded out of the folds of the woman man comes
    unfolded, and is always to come unfolded . . .

—Walt Whitman, "Unfolded Out of the Folds"

What aim had they, the Pair of Monks, in size
Enormous, dragged, while side by side they sate,
By panting steers up to this convent gate?

—William Wordsworth, "At the Eremite or Upper Convent of Camaldoli"

Is this, ye Gods, the Capitolian Hill?

—William Wordsworth, "At Rome"

Methinks that I could trip o'er heaviest soil,
Light as a buoyant bark from wave to wave,
Were mine the trusty staff that JEWEL gave
To youthful HOOKER . . .

—William Wordsworth, "Eminent Reformers"

Ah, when the Body, round which in love we clung,
Is chilled by death, does mutual service fail?

—William Wordsworth, "Other Influences"

Degenerate Douglas! oh, the unworthy Lord!

—William Wordsworth, "Sonnet, Composed at ——— Castle"

By antique Fancy trimmed—though lowly, bred
To dignity—in thee O SCHWYTZ! are seen
The genuine features of the golden mean . . .

—William Wordsworth, "The Town of Schwytz"

II

Disasters

Destruction lay on every side,
  Confusion, fire and despair;
No help, no hope, so they died,
  Two hundred people over there.

—Julia A. Moore,
"Ashtabula Disaster"

WILLIAM McGONAGALL (1830–1902)

For the laurels and bays of Greatest Bad Poet in the Language, Scotsmen (and many others) have no doubt that the true claimant is McGonagall. Even his detractors must admit to the epic sweep with which he manages whole-scale catastrophes. Bridge disasters, mining accidents, shipwrecks, and eight-alarm conflagrations send his pen effortlessly racing; and in his hands, grammar and syntax themselves sicken and die, and add to the litter of corpses.

William McGonagall, who always thought of himself as "Poet and Tragedian," was a handloom weaver in his native Dundee, where fellow workers seem to have egged him on to fancy himself a combination of geniuses. Evidently for laughs, they raised a quid to rent him a theater for a night, in which to perform his one-man interpretation of *Macbeth*, and applauded deafeningly. McGonagall, who had sold his topical poems as penny broadsheets, finally was encouraged to collect his *Poetic Gems* (Dundee, 1890). Reprinted in 1934, the book has been a steady seller ever since. It was followed by *More Poetic Gems* (Dundee and London, 1966), a posthumous collection of new manuscript discoveries in the Dundee Public Library.

A sweet and cheerful soul, even when reporting the slaughter of multitudes, McGonagall is capable of great range both in emotion and in matter.

The Albion Battleship Calamity

'Twas in the year of 1898, and on the 21st of June,
The launching of the Battleship Albion caused a
great gloom,

Amongst the relatives of many persons who were drowned in the River Thames,
Which their relatives will remember while life remains.

The vessel was christened by the Duchess of York,
And the spectators' hearts felt as light as cork
As the Duchess cut the cord that was holding the fine ship,
Then the spectators loudly cheered as the vessel slid down the slip.

The launching of the vessel was very well carried out,
While the guests on the stands cheered without any doubt,
Under the impression that everything would go well;
But, alas! instantaneously a bridge and staging fell.

Oh! little did the Duchess of York think that day
That so many lives would be taken away
At the launching of the good ship Albion,
But when she heard of the catastrophe she felt woe-begone.

But accidents will happen without any doubt,
And often the cause thereof is hard to find out;
And according to report, I've heard people say,
'Twas the great crowd on the bridge caused it to give way.

Just as the vessel entered the water the bridge and staging gave way,
Immersing some three hundred people which caused great dismay
Amongst thousands of spectators that were standing there,

And in the faces of the bystanders were depicted
despair.

Then the police boats instantly made for the fatal
spot,
And with the aid of dockyard hands several people
were got,
While some scrambled out themselves, the best way
they could—
And the most of them were the inhabitants of the
neighborhood.

Part of them were the wives and daughters of the
dockyard hands,
And as they gazed upon them they in amazement
stands;
And several bodies were hauled up quite dead.
Which filled the onlookers' hearts with pity and
dread.

One of the first rescued was a little baby,
Which was conveyed away to a mortuary;
And several were taken to the fitter's shed, and
attended to there
By the firemen and several nurses with the greatest
care.

Meanwhile heartrending scenes were taking place,
Whilst the tears ran down many a Mother and
Father's face,
That had lost their children in the River Thames,
Which they will remember while life remains.

Oh, Heaven! it was horrible to see the bodies laid
out in rows,
And as Fathers and Mothers passed along, adown
their cheeks the tears flows,

While their poor, sickly hearts were throbbing with
fear.

A great crowd had gathered to search for the missing
dead,
And many strong men broke down because their
heart with pity bled,
As they looked upon the distorted faces of their rela-
tives dear,
While adown their cheeks flowed many a silent tear.

The tenderest sympathy, no doubt, was shown to
them,
By the kind hearted Police and Firemen;
The scene in fact was most sickening to behold,
And enough to make one's blood run cold,
To see tear-stained men and women there
Searching for their relatives, and in their eyes a piti-
ful stare.

There's one brave man in particular I must mention,
And I'm sure he's worthy of the people's attention.
His name is Thomas Cooke, of No. 6 Percy Road,
Canning Town,
Who's name ought to be to posterity handed down,
Because he leapt into the River Thames, and hero-
ically did behave,
And rescued five persons from a watery grave.

Mr. Wilson, a young Electrician, got a terrible fright,
When he saw his mother and sister dead—he was
shocked at the sight,
Because his sister had not many days returned from
her honeymoon,
And in his countenance, alas! there was a sad gloom.

Her Majesty has sent a message of sympathy to the
bereaved ones in distress,

And the Duke and Duchess of York have sent 25 guineas I must confess,
And £1000 from the Directors of the Thames Ironworks and Shipbuilding Company,
Which I hope will help to fill the bereaved one's hearts with glee.

And in conclusion I will venture to say,
That accidents will happen by night and by day;
And I will say without any fear,
Because to me it appears quite clear,
That the stronger we our houses do build,
The less chance we have of being killed.

THOMAS HARDY (1840–1928)

When critics jumped with hobnailed boots upon his novel *Jude the Obscure* (1896), Thomas Hardy swore off prose and for the rest of his long life kept lyre-strumming. "The mutterings of the village atheist," G. K. Chesterton remarked, dismissing Hardy's work; but W. H. Auden, Philip Larkin, John Crowe Ransom, W. D. Snodgrass, and Dylan Thomas are among recent poets to love Hardy fiercely and (admittedly) to learn from him. If one is to read the *Collected Poems* with pleasure, he must see Hardy as a somewhat doddering old uncle, given to moments of clear genius and seasons of incompetence, whom one accepts for what he is, warts, tobacco-stains, and all. Notable are these lines on the loss of the good ship *Titanic*.

FROM The Convergence of the Twain

Dim moon-eyed fishes near
Gaze at the gilded gear

And query: "What does this vaingloriousness down
here?"

C. T. (fl. 1908)

"Gastric," published in a North Carolina newspaper over the initials "C. T." and now enshrined in Walser's *Nematodes in My Garden of Verse,* presents a peculiar problem to the connoisseur. The poem was obviously intended to be funny—and it is funny, especially when read aloud. But the suspicion grows that our laughter is on the wrong level, that it springs from watching the poem's humor so manifestly pass us by. So that (if we are right) a laugh over a poem like "Gastric" is to the laughter of ordinary humor as the sublime is to the merely beautiful.

Gastric

We stood at first before the mast
And watched the colors playing,
Of sunlight through the fog that passed
From wave-heads wildly spraying.

"We dreamed of this," the ladies cried,
"And when we woke were wishing
On this June morn that we might ride
At sea with you a-fishing!"

Our captain reefed his snowy sail
To aid us in our angling;
And 'long our lines, like coats of mail,
Bright flashed the fishes dangling.

As elm-boughs swing in Southern breeze
  When boughs with leaves are freighted,
So swayed our craft and crowned the seas
  And in the hollows waited.

The ladies felt a sinking void
  About the solar plexus;
My lassie said, with fun destroyed,
  "He reefed the sail to vex us."

She laid sad eyes on all the crew;
  She rolled them on the water;
Then back on me her eyes she threw—
  I wished I had not brought her.

(My vial-case was left ashore,
  So naught had I to give her;
I would have given my earthly store
  To have her on the river.)

With troubled breath she sighed and frowned
  As wrinkly as the ocean;
'Twas then she prayed for stable ground
  Instead of frothy motion.

With languid limbs she lay beside
  The vessel's kindly railing;
She hid her face, but could not hide
  Th' effect of ocean sailing.

For gastric muscles 'gan to play—
  Like crawfish ran their action—
And breakfast then was thrust away
  As by some stronger faction.

She rolled her eyes off to the land,
  Her beauty all seemed slaughtered;

No charming grace could she command,
  Her spirits were so watered.

She rose at length, but wilted yet
  Was this fair blooming daughter,
Who cast her lot with our gay set—
  Her bread upon the water.

FRANK ELWOOD SANFORD (fl. 1894)

This shaggy-dog poem first appeared in a book of *Wesleyan Verse* (Wesleyan University, Middletown, Conn., 1894). After its printing, the author seems to have disappeared into respectability.

The Outcast

See that wreck there in the gutter,
And those tattered clothes that flutter
                As the wind blows.

Age and hard times tell their story;
Youth's bright threads of future glory,
                Gone: poor fellow.

And the friends, once faithful whether
It was clear or stormy weather,
                Time has thinned those.

Now, alone, a tattered cloak on;
Poor, dilapidated, broken,—
                Old umbrella.

ANONYMOUS (fl. 1899)

The following stanza purports to be a translation from a sixteenth-century Turkish poet Abdulkerim. We have not checked its accuracy.

Dark Aspect and Prospect

Ah! cease to shroud the radiance of those cheeks,
  Those eyes that pale the lightnings of the opal!
An eclipse of the sun for days and weeks
  Forebodes disaster in Constantinople!

SYDNEY DOBELL (1824–1874)

Out of the "Spasmodic School" (a malicious but suggestive label fastened on them by William Edmondstoune Aytoun, whose parody *Firmilian, A Spasmodic Tragedy* (1854) demolished hope of their being taken seriously), several writers of interest have tottered. Among them, Sidney Dobell was described as "our most rising and sincere poet" by George Gilfillan, the School's best publicist. In the mid-1850s Dobell, before an audience of Edinburgh intellectuals, delivered himself of a lecture on the "Nature of Poetry" which (according to an account) "produced so serious an irritation of the chest, that his doctors ordered immediate change to a southern climate." Dobell's health was no whit aided in 1869 by his being rolled over upon by a horse.

The German Legion

In the cot beside the water,
In the white cot by the water,

The white cot by the white water,
There they laid the German maid.

There they wound her, singing round her,
Deftly wound her, singing round her,
Softly wound her, singing round her,
In a shroud like a cloud.

And they decked her as they wound her,
With a wreath of leaves they bound her,
Lornest leaves they scattered round her,
Singing grief with every leaf.

Singing grief with every leaf,
Sadder grief with sadder leaf,
Sweeter leaf with sweeter grief,
So 't was sung in a dark tongue.

Like a latter lily lying,
O'er whom falling leaves are sighing,
And autumn vapors crying,
Pale and cold on misty mould,

So I saw her sweet and lowly,
Shining shining pale and holy,
Thro' the dim woe slowly slowly,
Said and sung in that dark tongue.

Such an awe her beauty lent her,
While they sung I dared not enter
That charmed ring where she was centre,
But I stood with stirring blood

Till the song fell like a billow,
And I saw them leave her pillow,
And go forth to the far willow,
For the wreath of virgin death.

And I stood beside her pillow,
While they plucked the distant willow
And my heart rose like a billow
As I said to the pale dead—

"Oh, thou most fair and sweet virginity,
Of whom his heart that beats for thee doth know
Nor name nor story, that these limbs can be
For no man evermore, that thou must go
Cold to the cold, and that no eye shall see
That which thine unsolved womanhood doth owe
Of the incommunicable mystery
Shakes me with tears. I could kneel down by thee
And o'er thy chill unmarriageable rest
Cry, 'Thou who shalt no more at all be prest
To any heart, one moment come to this!
And feel me weeping with thy want of bliss,
And all the unpraised beauties of thy breast—
Thy breast which never shall a lover kiss!' "

Then I slowly left her pillow,
For they came back with the willow,
And my heart sinks as a billow
Doth implore towards the shore,

As I see the crown they weave her,
And I know that I must leave her,
And I feel that I could grieve her
Sad and sore for evermore.

And again they sang around her,
In a richer robe they wound her,
With the willow wreath they bound her,
And the loud song like a cloud

Of golden obscuration,
With the strange tongue of her nation,

Filled the house of lamentation,
Till she lay in melody,

Like a latter lily lying.
O'er whom falling leaves are sighing,
And the autumn vapors crying,
In a dream of evening gleam.

And I saw her sweet and lowly,
Shining shining pale and holy,
Thro' the dim woe slowly slowly
Said and sung in a dark tongue.

In the cot beside the water,
The white cot by the white water,
English cot by English water
That shall see the German sea.

WILLIAM McGONAGALL (1830–1902)

In the matter of disasters, McGonagall must be given the last word. The railroad bridge built over the Firth of Tay in 1877 would have been a notable triumph of design, had it not, eighteen months later, collapsed while a train was crossing it. Apparently it did not occur to the builder that a strong wind might cause additional stress. Dundee's great Poet and Tragedian was fortunately on hand to celebrate the bridge, the railroad, the disaster, and the replacement in 1887—by a different designer and some sixty feet upstream.

The Railway Bridge of the Silvery Tay

Beautiful Railway Bridge of the Silvery Tay!
With your numerous arches and pillars in so grand
  array,

And your central girders, which seem to the eye
To be almost towering to the sky.
The greatest wonder of the day.
And a great beautification to the River Tay,
Most beautiful to be seen,
Near by Dundee and the Magdalen Green.

Beautiful Railway Bridge of the Silvery Tay!
That has caused the Emperor of Brazil to leave
His home far away, *incognito* in his dress,
And view thee ere he passed along *en route* to
Inverness.

Beautiful Railway Bridge of the Silvery Tay!
The longest of the present day
That has ever crossed o'er a tidal river stream,
Most gigantic to be seen,
Near by Dundee and the Magdalen Green.

Beautiful Railway Bridge of the Silvery Tay!
Which will cause great rejoicing on the opening day,
And hundreds of people will come from far away,
Also the Queen, most gorgeous to be seen,
Near by Dundee and the Magdalen Green.

Beautiful Railway Bridge of the Silvery Tay!
And prosperity to Provost Cox, who has given
Thirty thousand pounds and upwards away
In helping to erect the Bridge of the Tay,
Most handsome to be seen,
Near by Dundee and the Magdalen Green.

Beautiful Railway Bridge of the Silvery Tay!
I hope that God will protect all passengers
By night and by day,
And that no accident will befall them while crossing
The Bridge of the Silvery Tay,

For that would be most awful to be seen
Near by Dundee and the Magdalen Green.

Beautiful Railway Bridge of the Silvery Tay!
And prosperity to Messrs Bouche and Grothe,
The famous engineers of the present day,
Who have succeeded in erecting the Railway
Bridge of the Silvery Tay,
Which stands unequalled to be seen
Near by Dundee and the Magdalen Green.

The Newport Railway

Success to the Newport Railway
Along the braes of the Silvery Tay,
And to Dundee straightway,
Across the Railway Bridge o' the Silvery Tay,
Which was opened on the 12th of May,
In the year of our Lord 1879,
Which will clear all expenses in a very short time
Because the thrifty housewives of Newport
To Dundee will often resort,
Which will be to them profit and sport,
By bringing cheap tea, bread, and jam,
And also some of Lipton's ham,
Which will make their hearts feel light and gay,
And cause them to bless the opening day
Of the Newport Railway.

The train is most beautiful to be seen,
With its long, white curling cloud of steam,
As the train passes on her way
Along the bonnie braes o' the Silvery Tay.

And if the people of Dundee
Should feel inclined to have a spree,

I am sure 'twill fill their hearts with glee
By crossing o'er to Newport,
And there they can have excellent sport,
By viewing the scenery beautiful and gay,
During the livelong summer day,

And then they can return at night
With spirits light and gay,
By the Newport Railway,
By night or by day,
Across the Railway Bridge o' the Silvery Tay.

Success to the undertakers of the Newport Railway,
Hoping the Lord will their labours repay,
And prove a blessing to the people
For many a long day
Who live near by Newport,
On the bonnie braes o' the Silvery Tay.

The Tay Bridge Disaster

Beautiful Railway Bridge of the Silv'ry Tay!
Alas! I am very sorry to say
That ninety lives have been taken away
On the last Sabbath day of 1879,
Which will be remember'd for a very long time.

'Twas about seven o'clock at night,
And the wind it blew with all its might,
And the rain came pouring down,
And the dark clouds seem'd to frown,
And the Demon of the air seem'd to say—
"I'll blow down the Bridge of Tay."

When the train left Edinburgh
The passengers' hearts were light and felt no sorrow,
But Boreas blew a terrific gale,

Which made their hearts for to quail,
And many of the passengers with fear did say—
"I hope God will send us safe across the Bridge of
Tay."

But when the train came near to Wormit Bay,
Boreas he did loud and angry bray,
And shook the central girders of the Bridge of Tay
On the last Sabbath day of 1879,
Which will be remember'd for a very long time.

So the train sped on with all its might,
And Bonnie Dundee soon hove in sight,
And the passengers' hearts felt light,
Thinking they would enjoy themselves on the New
Year,
With their friends at home they lov'd most dear,
And wish them all a happy New Year.

So the train mov'd slowly along the Bridge of Tay,
Until it was about midway,
Then the central girders with a crash gave way,
And down went the train and passengers into the
Tay!
The Storm Fiend did loudly bray,
Because ninety lives had been taken away,
On the last Sabbath day of 1879,
Which will be remember'd for a very long time.

As soon as the catastrophe came to be known
The alarm from mouth to mouth was blown,
And the cry rang out all o'er the town,
Good Heavens! the Tay Bridge is blown down,
And a passenger train from Edinburgh,
Which fill'd all the people's hearts with sorrow,
And made them for to turn pale,

Because none of the passengers were sav'd to tell the tale
How the disaster happen'd on the last Sabbath day of 1879
Which will be remember'd for a very long time.

It must have been an awful sight,
To witness in the dusky moonlight,
While the Storm Fiend did laugh, and angry did bray,
Along the Railway Bridge of the Silv'ry Tay.
Oh! ill-fated Bridge of the Silv'ry Tay,
I must now conclude my lay
By telling the world fearlessly without the least dismay,
That your central girders would not have given way,
At least many sensible men do say,
Had they been supported on each side with buttresses,
At least many sensible men confesses,
For the stronger we our houses do build,
The less chance we have of being killed.

An Address to the New Tay Bridge

Beautiful new railway bridge of the Silvery Tay,
With your strong brick piers and buttresses in so grand array,
And your thirteen central girders, which seem to my eye
Strong enough all windy storms to defy.
And as I gaze upon thee my heart feels gay,
Because thou are the greatest railway bridge of the present day,
And can be seen for miles away
From north, south, east, or west of the Tay
On a beautiful and clear sunshiny day,

And ought to make the hearts of the "Mars" boys feel gay,
Because thine equal nowhere can be seen,
Only near by Dundee and the bonnie Magdalen Green.

Beautiful new railway bridge of the Silvery Tay,
With thy beautiful side-screens along your railway,
Which will be a great protection on a windy day,
So as the railway carriages won't be blown away,
And ought to cheer the hearts of the passengers night and day
As they are conveyed along thy beautiful railway,
And towering above the silvery Tay,
Spanning the beautiful river shore to shore
Upwards of two miles and more,
Which is most wonderful to be seen
Near by Dundee and the bonnie Magdalen Green.

Thy structure to my eye seems strong and grand,
And the workmanship most skillfully planned;
And I hope the designers, Messrs Barlow & Arrol, will prosper for many a day
For erecting thee across the beautiful Tay.
And I think nobody need have the least dismay
To cross o'er thee by night or by day,
Because thy strength is visible to be seen
Near by Dundee and the bonnie Magdalen Green.

Beautiful new railway bridge of the Silvery Tay,
I wish you success for many a year and a day,
And I hope thousands of people will come from far away,
Both high and low without delay,
From the north, south, east, and the west,
Because as a railway bridge thou are the best;

Thou standest unequalled to be seen
Near by Dundee and the bonnie Magdalen Green.

And for beauty thou art most lovely to be seen
As the train crosses o'er thee with her cloud of steam;
And you look well, painted the colour of marone,
And to find thy equal there is none,
Which, without fear of contradiction, I venture to
say,
Because you are the longest railway bridge of the
present day
That now crosses o'er a tidal river stream,
And the most handsome to be seen
Near by Dundee and the bonnie Magdalen Green.

The New Yorkers boast about their Brooklyn Bridge,
But in comparison to thee it seems like a midge,
Because thou spannest the silvery Tay
A mile and more longer I venture to say;
Besides the railway carriages are pulled across by a
rope,
Therefore Brooklyn Bridge cannot with thee cope;
And as you have been opened on the 20th day of
June,
I hope Her Majesty Queen Victoria will visit thee
very soon,
Because thou are worthy of a visit from Duke, Lord,
or Queen,
And strong and securely built, which is most worthy
to be seen
Near by Dundee and the bonnie Magdalen Green.

III

Love, Mostly Erotic

I clasp her with fierceness and passion,
  And kiss her with shudder and groan.
    —Ella Wheeler Wilcox,
    "Delilah"

Droop, droop, soft little eyelids!
  Droop over eyes of weird wild blue!
Under the fringe of those tremulous shy lids,
  Glances of fun and of love leak through!
    —Mortimer Collins,
    "Droop, Droop!"

COVENTRY PATMORE (1823–1896)

Patmore was a supernumerary assistant in the British Museum when he published the various parts of *The Angel in the House,* Victorian England's best-loved domestic poem. (The excerpts which follow are from Canto III, where the lover meets his Angel, Honoria.) There are in Patmore's work enough felicities to justify the enthusiasm of as discerning a critic as John Heath-Stubbs. And then there are the dead spots that Saintsbury noticed: "When a man writes—

> Our witnesses the cook and groom,
> We signed the lease for seven years more,

it is not unreasonable to think that Apollo, if he thought it worth his while, must have twitched the poet's ear rather sharply and that attention should have been paid to the twitch." After the death of his first wife in 1862, Patmore changed his religion, took on a new wife, got a fortune with the wife, retired to Sussex, began the practice of strolling by the sea, and wrote his best work, *To the Unknown Eros.* As he himself is reported to have said more than once, "Coventry is a clever fellow."

FROM *The Angel in the House*

He prays for some hard thing to do,
  Some work of fame and labour immense,
To stretch the languid bulk and thew
  Of love's fresh-born magnipotence.
      ("The Lover," Canto III: Honoria)

Grown weary with a week's exile
  From those fair friends, I rode to see

The church-restorings; lounged awhile,
  And met the Dean; was ask'd to tea,
And found their cousin, Frederick Graham,
  At Honor's side. Was I concern'd,
If, when she sang, his colour came,
  That mine, as with a buffet, burn'd?
A man to please a girl! thought I,
  Retorting his forced smiles, the shrouds
Of wrath, so hid as she was by,
Sweet moon between her lighted clouds!
("Honoria," Canto III: Honoria)

ROBERT BROWNING (1812–1889)

Though much of his old age was spent in being lionized, Browning today is probably best known for running off with Elizabeth Barrett and occasioning a popular play and a Virginia Woolf novel seen through the watery gaze of a pet cocker spaniel. In our century, he has exerted his influence on the work of poets from Ezra Pound and Philip Larkin down to Frederick Fanning Ayer; but works such as the book-length monologue *Prince Hohenstiel-Schwangau, Saviour of Society* (1871) perhaps are read less now than they once were. In his last years, Browning—to quote a recent editor, Donald Smalley—"was all too frequently guilty of garrulity." The following excerpt from "In a Gondola," in the *Dramatic Lyrics* of 1842, suggests that some enduring qualities of his work were present early.

FROM In A Gondola

He sings.

I

Past we glide, and past, and past!
  What's that poor Agnese doing
Where they make the shutters fast?
  Gray Zanobi's just a-wooing
To his couch the purchased bride:
  Past we glide!

II

Past we glide, and past, and past!
  Why's the Pucci Palace flaring
Like a beacon to the blast?
  Guests by hundreds, not one caring
If the dear host's neck were wried:
  Past we glide!

She sings.

I

The moth's kiss, first!
Kiss me as if you made believe
You were not sure, this eve,
How my face, your flower, had pursed
Its petals up; so, here and there
You brush it, till I grow aware
Who wants me, and wide ope I burst.

II

The bee's kiss, now!
Kiss me as if you entered gay
My heart at some noonday,
A bud that dares not disallow
The claim, so all is rendered up,

And passively its shattered cup
Over your head to sleep I bow.

He sings.

I

What are we two?
I am a Jew,
And carry thee, farther than friends can pursue,
To a feast of our tribe;
Where they need thee to bribe
The devil that blasts them unless he imbibe
Thy . . . Scatter the vision forever! And now,
As of old, I am I, thou art thou!

II

Say again, what we are?
The sprite of a star,
I lure thee above where the destinies bar
My plumes their full play
Till a ruddier ray
Than my pale one announce there is withering away
Some . . . Scatter the vision forever! And now,
As of old, I am I, thou art thou!

. . . .

He speaks, musing.

Lie back; could thought of mine improve you?
From this should let there spring
A wing; from this, another wing;
Wings, not legs and feet, shall move you!
Snow-white must they spring, to blend
With your flesh, but I intend
They shall deepen to the end,
Broader, into burning gold,

Till both wings crescent-wise enfold
Your perfect self, from 'neath your feet
To o'er your head, where, lo, they meet
As if a million sword-blades hurled
Defiance from you to the world!

Rescue me thou, the only real!
And scare away this mad ideal
That came, nor motions to depart!
Thanks! Now, stay ever as thou art!

EMILY DICKINSON (1830–1886)

Emily Dickinson's habit of stowing her poems in an attic trunk, tied in little packets, may have delayed her fame; but in many a poem she seems pretty sure that fame was going to catch up with her. Some quality inherent in her work (perhaps her punctuation) seems always to have made editors itch to rewrite her. Even in her lifetime, it was a high-handed local newspaper editor whose revisions first drove her to attic trunks. Reading her at last through the clear glass of Thomas H. Johnson's magnificent edition, one nevertheless agrees at times with Robert Hillyer: "Surely our sprite who over Amherst hovered/Would gain if no more poems were discovered." Perplexed and divided, the present editors could not agree on a pigeonhole for the following poem, which some thought not merely erotic, but inspirational.

'He was weak'

He was weak, and I was strong—then—
So He let me lead him in—

I was weak, and He was strong then—
So I let him lead me—Home.

'Twasn't far—the door was near—
'Twasn't dark—for He went—too—
'Twasn't loud, for He said nought—
That was all I cared to know.

Day knocked—and we must part—
Neither—was strongest—now—
He strove—and I strove—too—
We did'nt do it—tho'!

HARRY EDWARD MILLS (fl. 1901)

In his *Select Sunflowers* (Fort Scott, Kansas, 1901), Mills cultivates a familiar garden of folksy sentiment, distinguished by a few western perennials. Squaws and papooses lend him opportunities for heart-throbs not available to Edgar A. Guest, back in Detroit; and in a ballad, "The Cowboy Poet," we are told of a gun-slinger who, by sending a few bullets under the dancing feet of his local newspaper editor, promptly has his verses accepted for publication:

In life's uncertain contest brass helps many men ahead,
But when it comes to poets nothing takes the place of lead.

Select Sunflowers is all lead and a mile wide.

FROM On a Rainy Night

My love tonight is far away;
  And I am sad and lonely;
My restive spirit night and day
  Is longing for her only.

I see her in my fondest moods,
  She haunts the parlor hallway;
And yet her form my clasp eludes,
  Her lips my kisses alway.

ELLA WHEELER WILCOX (1850–1919)

It is a curious quirk that when these stanzas first appeared they seemed as bad as they do today. At the time, however, they were denounced for moral reasons. Shrewdly, their publisher had sent copies of Ella Wheeler's *Poems of Passion* (Chicago, 1883) to every self-appointed custodian of the public virginity who could be depended on to be outraged by it. Despite an accusation in the New York *Sun* that the author must be some "half-tipsy wanton," it emerged that Miss Wheeler was a farm girl from Johnson Centre, Wisconsin, whose acquaintance with vice and satiety had been confined to a few visits to Madison and to the novels of Mrs. E. D. E. N. Southworth. Her royalties soon enabled her to get married, put a new roof on the old homestead, and buy her father a Sunday suit. "Laugh, and the world laughs with you;/Weep, and you weep alone," are her most famous lines. These must be her most infamous.

FROM The Farewell of Clarimonde

Adieu, Romauld! But thou canst not forget me,
Although no more I haunt thy dreams at night,
Thy hungering heart forever must regret me,
And starve for those lost moments of delight.

Naught shall avail thy priestly rites and duties—
Nor fears of Hell, nor hope of Heaven beyond:

Before the Cross shall rise my fair form's beauties—
The lips, the limbs, the eyes of Clarimonde.

I knew all arts of love: he who possessed me
Possessed all women, and could never tire:
A new life dawned for him who once caressed me:
Satiety itself I set on fire.

Inconstancy I chained: men died to win me;
Kings cast by crowns for one hour on my breast,
And all the passionate tide of love within me
I gave to thee, Romauld. Wert thou not blest?

ALICE MEYNELL (1850–1923)

For almost twenty years Mrs. Meynell, a woman of vast generosity, helped fill the columns of her husband's newspaper while tending seven children and that broken-down genius, Francis Thompson, a perpetual houseguest, whom she persuaded to swear off laudanum. She hardly deserves the anonymous clerihew:

Alice Meynell
Was frequently banal.
She served Francis Thompson
To take his romps on.

True, however, her ecstasies occasionally soared off into outer space. As her child, Monica, put it in a letter to her:

Dear Mother,—I hope you will in time give up your absurd thoughts about literature. It makes my mind quite feverish when I think of the exhaltation your undergoing. . . . Just because Mr. Henley and those sort of unsencere men say you write well simply because they know if they don't flatter you they'll never get anything for their paper. Now mother take my advise and don't be quite so ecstatic, you'll get on just as well in the world . . .

The Shepherdess

She walks—the lady of my delight—
  A shepherdess of sheep.
Her flocks are thoughts. She keeps them white;
  She guards them from the steep;
She feeds them on the fragrant height,
  And folds them in for sleep.

She roams maternal hills and bright,
  Dark valleys safe and deep.
Into that tender breast at night
  The chastest stars may peep.
She walks—the lady of my delight—
  A shepherdess of sheep.

She holds her little thoughts in sight,
  Though gay they run and leap.
She is so circumspect and right;
  She has her soul to keep.
She walks—the lady of my delight—
  A shepherdess of sheep.

JOHN CLEVELAND (1613–1658)

Royalist and Cambridge wit, Cleveland was dealt such a critical blow by Dr. Johnson that his stock seems never to have recovered. Things were not always so. Twenty-five editions of his poems were issued before 1700, and his skill at growing ingenious conceits was widely admired and emulated. Cleveland's talent for bombast served him well when, after three months in Yarmouth Prison, he wrote to Oliver Cromwell asking to be released. According to a contemporary, he composed "an address to the Pageant Power at Whitehall of so much gallant reason and so much towering language as looked bigger than his Highness, shrinking before the Majesty of his pen." (The letter worked.) "We cannot read a verse of Cleveland's," said John Dryden, "without making a face at it, as if every word were a pill to swallow."

To the State of Love, or, The Senses' Festival

I saw a vision yesternight
Enough to sate a seeker's sight:
I wished my self a Shaker there
And her quick pants my trembling sphere.
It was a she so glittering bright
You'd think her soul an Adamite;
A person of so rare a frame
Her body might be lined with th' same.
Beauty's chiefest maid of honor,
You may break Lent with looking on her.
  Not the fair Abbess of the skies,
  With all her nunnery of eyes,
  Can show me such a glorious prize.

And yet, because 'tis more renown
To make a shadow shine, she's brown;
A brown for which Heaven would disband
The galaxy, and stars be tanned;
Brown by reflection, as her eye
Deals out the summer's livery.
Old dormant windows must confess
Her beams; their glimmering spectacles,
Struck with the splendor of her face,
Do th' office of a burning-glass.
  Now where such radiant lights have shown,
  No wonder if her cheeks be grown
  Sun-burnt with luster of her own.

My sight took pay, but (thank my charms)
I now empale her in mine arms,
(Love's compasses) confining you,
Good Angels, to a circle too.
Is not the Universe strait-laced
When I can clasp it in the waist?
My amorous folds about thee hurled,
With Drake I girdle in the world.
I hoop the firmament and make
This my embrace the zodiac.
  How would thy center take my sense
  When admiration doth commence
  At the extreme circumference?

Now to the melting kiss that sips
The jellied philter of her lips;
So sweet, there is no tongue can phrase 't,
Till transubstantiate with a taste.
Inspired like Mahomet from above
By the billing of my heav'nly dove,
Love prints his signets in her smacks,
Those ruddy drops of squeezing wax,
Which, wheresoever she imparts,
They're privvy seals to take up hearts.
  Our mouths encountering at the sport,
  My slippery soul had quit the fort,
  But that she stopped the sally-port.

Next to those sweets, her lips dispense
(As twin-conserves of eloquence)
The sweet perfume her breath affords,
Incorporating with her words.
No rosary this Votress needs,
Her very syllables are beads.
No sooner 'twixt those rubies born,
But jewels are in ear-rings worn.

With what delight her speech doth enter,
It is a kiss of the second venter.
And I dissolve at what I hear
As if another Rosamond were
Couched in the labyrinth of my ear.

Yet that's but a preludious bliss,
Two souls pickearing in a kiss.
Embraces do but draw the line,
'Tis storming that must take her in.
When bodies join and victory hovers
'Twixt the equal fluttering lovers,
This is the game; make stakes my dear,
Hark how the sprightly chanticleer,
That Baron Tell-clock of the night,
Sounds boot-esel to Cupid's knight.
Then have at all, the pass is got,
For coming off, oh name it not:
Who would not die upon the spot?

FRED EMERSON BROOKS (fl. 1894)

Brooks, who may or may not have been kin to the Sage of Concord, was the author of *Old Ace and Other Poems*, *Pickett's Charge*, and other popular verse-volumes of the late nineteenth century. As a reader of his work (mostly on heroic, patriotic, and erotic themes), he was reported able to bring an audience to its feet with cheers.

FROM Kissing

Those lustrous eyes but tell me this,
What modest lips would ne'er impart:
He does not steal who takes a kiss,
But makes a curtsey to the heart.

GEORGE WITHER (1588–1667)

One of the more effusive poets of the seventeenth century, Wither basked in early popularity. A volume of satire, however—*Abuses Stript and Whipt*—got him thrown into jail. In his middle years he took to Puritanism and hymn-writing. During the Civil War he was a Captain of Horse in the Puritan army and the great old gossip John Aubrey tells us he was "taken prisoner, and was in danger of his Life, having written severely against the King, &c. Sir John Denham went to the King, and desired his Majestie not to hang him, for that *whilst G. W. lived, he* [Denham] *should not be the worst Poet in England.*"

FROM Philarete to his Mistress

Thee entirely I have loved,
  So thy sweetness on me wrought;
Yet thy beauty never moved
  Ill temptations in my thought,
    But still did thy beauty's ray,
    Sun-like, drive those fogs away.

. . . .

Thou to no man favour deignest
  But what's fitting to bestow;
Neither servants entertainest
  That can ever wanton grow;
    For the more they look on thee,
    Their desires still bettered be.

This thy picture, therefore, show I
  Naked unto every eye,
Yet no fear of rival know I,

Neither touch of jealousy;
For the more make love to thee,
I the more shall pleased be.

I am no Italian lover
That will mew thee in a jail;
But thy beauty I discover,
English-like, without a veil.
If thou may'st be won away,
Win and wear thee he that may.

WILLIAM ERNEST HENLEY (1849–1903)

Henley, most famous for a sanguine claim of being the captain of his own soul, was the model for Captain John Silver in Robert Louis Stevenson's *Treasure Island*. He was also a staunch supporter of the Boer War and of the poetry of T. E. Brown.

Orientale

She's an enchanting little Israelite,
A world of hidden dimples!—Dusky-eyed,
A starry-glancing daughter of the Bride,
With hair escaped from some Arabian Night,
Her lip is red, her cheek is golden-white,
Her nose a scimitar; and, set aside
The bamboo hat she cocks with so much pride,
Her dress a dream of daintiness and delight.
And when she passes with the dreadful boys
And romping girls, the cockneys loud and crude,
My thought, to the Minories tied yet moved to range
The Land o' the Sun, commingles with the noise

Of magian drums and scents of sandalwood
A touch Sidonian—modern—taking—strange!

THOMAS MOORE (1779–1852)

When a critic named Jeffrey threw off on Moore's poems, Moore challenged him to a duel. When Byron ridiculed that duel (which never took place) in *English Bards, and Scotch Reviewers,* Moore challenged Byron to a duel. It never took place either.

To Cara, After an Interval of Absence

Concealed within the shady wood
  A mother left her sleeping-child,
And flew to cull her rustic food,
  The fruitage of the forest wild.

But storms upon her pathway rise,
  The mother roams, astray and weeping,
Far from the weak appealing cries
  Of him she left so sweetly sleeping.

She hopes, she fears—a light is seen,
  And gentler blows the night-wind's breath;
Yet no—'tis gone—the storms are keen,
  The baby may be chilled to death!

Perhaps his little eyes are shaded
  Dim by Death's eternal chill—
And yet, perhaps, they are not faded;
  Life and love may light them still.

Thus, when my soul with parting sigh,
  Hung on thy hand's bewildering touch,

And, timid, asked that speaking eye,
  If parting pained thee half so much:

I thought, and, oh! forgive the thought,
  For who, by eyes like thine inspired,
Could e'er resist the flattering fault
  Of fancying what his soul desired?

Yes—I *did* think, in Cara's mind,
  Though yet to Cara's mind unknown,
I left one infant wish behind,
  One feeling, which I called my own!

Oh blest! though but in fancy blest,
  How did I ask of pity's care,
To shield and strengthen in thy breast
  The nursling I had cradled there.

And, many an hour beguiled by pleasure,
  And many an hour of sorrow numbering,
I ne'er forgot the new-born treasure
  I left within thy bosom slumbering.

Perhaps indifference has not chilled it,
  Haply it yet a throb may give—
Yet no—perhaps a doubt has killed it!
  Oh, Cara!—*does* the infant live?

ARTHUR HUGH CLOUGH (1819–1861)

Clough is best known for a poem not quite bad enough for the present collection, "Say Not the Struggle Naught Availeth." His eccentric poem-cycle *Amours de Voyage*—in what he called "anglo-savage hexameters"—deserves more notice. He married a cousin of

Florence Nightingale and died of malaria. Matthew Arnold commemorated his passing in the poem "Thyrsis."

Les Vaches

The skies have sunk and hid the upper snow,
Home, Rose, and home, Provence and La Palie,
The rainy clouds are filing fast below,
And wet will be the path, and wet shall we.
Home, Rose, and home, Provence and La Palie.

Ah dear, and where is he, a year agone
Who stepped beside and cheered us on and on?
My sweetheart wanders far away from me,
In foreign land or o'er a foreign sea.
Home, Rose, and home, Provence and La Palie.

The lightning zigzags shot across the sky,
(Home, Rose, and home, Provence and La Palie,)
And through the vale the rains go sweeping by,
Ah me, and when in shelter shall we be?
Home, Rose, and home, Provence and La Palie.

Cold, dreary cold, the stormy winds feel they
O'er foreign lands and foreign seas that stray.
(Home, Rose, and home, Provence and La Palie.)
And doth he e'er, I wonder, bring to mind
The pleasant huts and herds he left behind?
And doth he sometimes in his slumbering see
The feeding kine, and doth he think of me,
My sweetheart wandering wheresoe'er it be?
Home, Rose, and home, Provence and La Palie.

The thunder bellows far from snow to snow,
(Home, Rose, and home, Provence and La Palie)

And loud and louder roars the flood below.
Heigh ho! but soon in shelter shall we be.
Home, Rose, and home, Provence and La Palie.

Or shall he find before his term be sped,
Some comelier maid that he shall wish to wed?
(Home, Rose, and home, Provence and La Palie,)
For weary is work, and weary day by day
To have your comfort miles on miles away.
Home, Rose, and home, Provence and La Palie.
Or may it be 'tis I shall find my mate,
And he returning see himself too late?
For work we must, and what we see, we see,
And God he knows, and what must be, must be,
When sweethearts wander far away from me.
Home, Rose, and home, Provence and La Palie.

The sky behind is brightening up anew,
(Home, Rose, and home, Provence and La Palie),
The rain is ending, and our journey too;
Heigh ho! aha! for here at home are we:—
In, Rose, and in Provence and La Palie.

ALFRED, LORD TENNYSON (1809–1892)

Tennyson wrote his first poems at the age of 5 and continued writing into his 80s. He was convinced very early that his soul had become "godlike."

Yea! in that hour I could have fallen down
Before my own strong soul and worshipp'd it.

From then on, he spoke "in God's name" and later complained of feeling like "a priest who can never leave the sanctuary." In 1850 he succeeded Wordsworth as poet laureate. "Lilian" is an early effort.

Lilian

I

Airy, fairy Lilian,
Flitting, fairy Lilian,
When I ask her if she love me,
Claps her tiny hands above me,
Laughing all she can;
She'll not tell me if she love me,
Cruel little Lilian.

II

When my passion seeks
Pleasance in love-sighs,
She, looking thro' and thro' me
Thoroughly to undo me,
Smiling, never speaks:
So innocent-arch, so cunning-simple,
From beneath her purfled wimple
Glancing with black-beaded eyes,
Till the lightning laughters dimple
The baby-roses in her cheeks;
Then away she flies.

III

Prythee weep, May Lilian!
Gaiety without eclipse
Wearieth me, May Lilian;
Thro' my very heart it thrilleth
When from crimson-threaded lips
Silver-treble laughter trilleth:
Prythee weep, May Lilian!

IV

Praying all I can,
If prayers will not hush thee,
Airy Lilian,

Like a rose-leaf I will crush thee,
    Fairy Lilian.

ALI SEDAT HILMI TÖREL (b. 1930)

Author, poet, journalist, translator, and publisher, A. S. H. Törel is now Chief of the Foreign Relations Division, Scientific and Technical Research Council of Turkey, in Ankara. In kindly granting us permission to include lines penned while he was yet a student at the American Academy, Larnaca, Cyprus, Törel noted that he has written ten books in Turkish and English. His other poetry volumes in English include *Pearls* (1957) and *Hated Souvenirs and Hope* (1960), published by Messrs. Arthur H. Stockwell, Ltd., Devon, U.K.; and *Massacre of Turks on Christmas Day* (1964). Still another, *The Old Man and the Snake*, is promised.

Although Törel's work may have matured since *Verse at Random* (Larnaca, 1953), from which "My Indian Girl" is taken, it is impossible not to be engaged by the author's tone of youthful dedication. "*Verse at Random*," he declares in his preface, "is published despite all the soaking discouragement of so many wet blankets all around it. . . . Machines or beasts may not appreciate or care to have a look at any kind of poetry. But those who are human—and there are many still—will not dismiss any kind of verse or poetry. It is my hope that *Verse at Random* will speak to its readers at random."

My Indian Girl

I trail and trail along the mountain range,
I am in search of yellow iron, that is gold;

I tell my story which is not so very strange,
By singing on the trail far off the fold!
O lei, O lei, O lei . . .

Back in a green, green valley by the lake,
I kissed my Indian girl by accident;
Long was her hair to bind me at the stake,
I met the flames of love, my heart was rent!
O lei, O lei, O lei . . .

Her name was Golden Luck, her eyes were black;
Her voice was sweeter than a nightingale's!
So fascinating was our secret smack,
We joined our hearts and rode on common trails!
O lei, O lei, O lei . . .

CHARLES OTIS JUDKINS (fl. 1894)

From *Wesleyan Verse*, again, comes one aspect of undergraduate love in Middletown, Connecticut.

The Play

The full moon hung above the sea;
We leaned against the vessel's rail
And watched a moonbeam kiss the sail.
The full moon hung above the sea.

The full moon sank beneath the sea;
The play went on beside the rail:
My role "The Moonbeam"; hers "The Sail."
The full moon sank beneath the sea.

WILLIAM WORDSWORTH (1770–1850)

By the time Wordsworth was appointed Poet Laureate in 1843, he had outlived two generations of Romantic poets and his own talent. A longer literary senility has never been recorded. "Ellen Irwin," however, was written in his prime and published in 1800, just two years after "Tintern Abbey."

Ellen Irwin: or, The Braes of Kirtle

Fair Ellen Irwin, when she sate
Upon the braes of Kirtle,
Was lovely as a Grecian maid
Adorned with wreaths of myrtle;
Young Adam Bruce beside her lay,
And there did they beguile the day
With love and gentle speeches,
Beneath the budding beeches.

From many knights and many squires
The Bruce had been selected;
And Gordon, fairest of them all,
By Ellen was rejected.
Sad tidings to that noble Youth!
For it may be proclaimed with truth,
If Bruce hath loved sincerely,
That Gordon loves as dearly.

But what are Gordon's form and face,
His shattered hopes and crosses,
To them, 'mid Kirtle's pleasant braes,
Reclined on flowers and mosses?
Alas that ever he was born!
The Gordon, couched behind a thorn,
Sees them and their caressing;
Beholds them blest and blessing.

Proud Gordon, maddened by the thoughts
That through his brain are travelling,
Rushed forth, and at the heart of Bruce
He launched a deadly javelin!
Fair Ellen saw it as it came,
And, starting up to meet the same,
Did with her body cover
The Youth, her chosen lover.

And, falling into Bruce's arms,
Thus died the beauteous Ellen,
Thus, from the heart of her True-love,
The mortal spear repelling.
And Bruce, as soon as he had slain
The Gordon, sailed away to Spain;
And fought with rage incessant
Against the Moorish crescent.

But many days, and many months,
And many years ensuing,
This wretched Knight did vainly seek
The death that he was wooing.
So, coming his last help to crave,
Heart-broken, upon Ellen's grave
His body he extended,
And there his sorrow ended.

Now ye, who willingly have heard
The tale I have been telling,
May in Kirkconnell churchyard view
The grave of lovely Ellen:
By Ellen's side the Bruce is laid;
And, for the stone upon his head,
May no rude hand deface it,
And its forlorn *Hic jacet!*

ANONYMOUS (fl. 1829)

This climactic stanza comes from an opus in J. Grigg's *Southern and Western Songster* (Philadelphia, 1829). "The galley slave," observes George Stuyvesant Jackson (who quotes it in his *Early Songs of Uncle Sam*), "evidently becomes brain-weary after much ardent and confusing exposition."

FROM The Galley Slave

"How fortune deceives! I had pleasure in tow,
  The port where she dwelt we'd in view;
But the wish'd nuptial morn was o'erclouded with
    woe,
  And, dear Anna, I was hurried from you.
Our shallop was boarded, and I was borne away
  To behold my dear Anna no more;
But despair wastes my spirits, my form feels decay—"
  He sigh'd, and expired at the oar.

IV

Family and Marriage

> "Not a day passes, not a minute or second without an accouchement"
>
> —W. Whitman,
> "To Think of Time"

DR. A. RASHEED GHAZI (fl. 1970)

Apparently intended as a work of popular education, this poem was composed by Dr. Ghazi while he was serving as Joint Director of the West Pakistan Research and Evaluation Center in Lahore.

A Poem on Inter-Uterine Device

Under the most ideal remedy,
Who cares to have an IUD,

Most modern method of contraception,
Gives nearly 98% of protection,

Bleeding, spotting and cramps are some,
More than half the battle is won.

To get an IUD fitted is a simple matter,
Just the time one takes to sip a glass of water,

Just get hold of the village "dai,"
And walk to the Health Center nearby.

Nothing is charged, service is free,
Follow-up is essential, don't you agree?

Once inserted can stay for years,
Couples enjoy without any fear,

Loaded once, repetition is none,
Unlike the double barrel gun.

Easy to handle and effective on the whole,
To get it fitted should be married women's goal

If one wants, can get a trial free,
Just who cares to come with me.

STEPHEN TROPP (b. 1930)

Tropp's quatrain is the opening work in *Beat Coast East, An Anthology of Rebellion* (New York, 1960), published by the Excelsior Press. As the editor, Stanley Fisher, remarks in his preface, "The maelstroms of feelings and escutcheons of obscenity in this book are the incorrigible American apostasies of the nouveau Minute Man—in his incubus struggle to retain his incommunicable vision against the minotaur of suburban dullness and fear."

My Wife Is My Shirt

My wife is my shirt
I put my hands through her armpits
slide my head through her mouth
& finally button her blood around my hands

THOMAS HARDY (1840–1928)

FROM A Jog-trot Pair

Trite usages in tamest style
Had tended to their plighting.
"It's just worth while,
Perhaps," they had said. "And saves much sad good-
nighting."

And petty seemed the happenings
That ministered to their joyance:
Simple things,
Onerous to satiate souls, increased their buoyance.

ALFRED AUSTIN (1835–1913)

To the astonishment of his contemporaries, Austin in 1896 was appointed Poet Laureate—because, as Lord Salisbury later confessed, "nobody else had applied." Love of country and love of countryside are his obsessing themes. Poem after poem conjures an England safe and steady, Victoria on her throne; while throstles jostle and mate, amid the occasional scream of a yaffel. On the one hand, Austin laments the decline of ancient virtues, and deplores gold-grabbing ("Tarpeia's doom be thine; / And perish smothered in a grave of gold"); while on the other, he watches with zeal the extension of Empire ("And Ganges jewels the Imperial Crown / That girds her brow"). Undivided, however, is his confidence that "Nothing can match, where'er we roam, / An English wife in an English home."

To Beatrice Stuart Wortley: AETAT 2

I

Patter, patter, little feet,
Making music quaint and sweet,
Up the passage, down the stair;
Patter, patter everywhere.

II

Ripple, ripple little voice;
When I hear you, I rejoice.
When you cease to crow and coo
Then my heart grows silent too.

III

Frolic, frolic, little form,
While the day is young and warm,
When the shadows shun the west,
Climb up to my knee, and rest.

IV

Slumber, slumber, little head,
Gambols o'er and night prayers said.
I will give you in your cot
Kisses that awake you not.

V

Open, open little lids!
Lambs are frisking in the meads;
Blackcaps flit from stem to stem;
Come and chirp along with them.

VI

Change not, change not, little fay;
Still be as you are to-day.
What a loss is growth of sense,
With decrease of innocence!

VII

Something in your little ways
Wins me more than love or praise.
You have gone, and I feel still
Void I somehow cannot fill.

VIII

Yes, you leave, when you depart
Empty cradle in my heart,
Where I sit and rock my pain,
Singing lullaby in rain.

IX

Come back, come back, little feet
Bring again the music sweet
To the garden, to the stair;
Patter, chatter everywhere.

WILLIAM MORRIS (1834–1896)

Painter, architect, designer of wallpaper and chintz, poet, novelist, printer, captain of a very small but important industry, the man who fashioned the Morris chair also wrote *The Earthly Paradise*, which may just be the longest poem in the English language.

Old Love

"You must be very old, Sir Giles,"
  I said; he said: "Yea, very old:"
Whereat the mournfullest of smiles
  Creased his dry skin with many a fold.

"They hammer'd out my basnet point
  Into a round salade," he said,
"The basnet being quite out of joint,
  Natheless the salade rasps my head."

He gazed at the great fire awhile:
  "And you are getting old, Sir John;"
(He said this with that cunning smile
  That was most sad;) "we both wear on,

"Knights come to court and look at me,
  With eyebrows up, except my lord,
And my dear lady, none I see
  That know the ways of my old sword."

(My lady! at that word no pang
  Stopp'd all my blood.) "But tell me, John
Is it quite true that pagans hang
  So thick about the east, that on

"The eastern sea no Venice flag
  Can fly unpaid for?" "True," I said,

"And in such way the miscreants drag
  Christ's cross upon the ground, I dread

"That Constantine must fall this year."
  Within my heart; "These things are small;
This is not small, that things outwear
  I thought were made for ever, yea, all,

"All things go soon or late;" I said—
  I saw the duke in court next day;
Just as before, his grand great head
  Above his gold robes dreaming lay,

Only his face was paler; there
  I saw his duchess sit by him;
And she—she was changed more; her hair
  Before my eyes that used to swim,

And make me dizzy with great bliss
  Once when I used to watch her sit—
Her hair is bright still, yet it is
  As though some dust were thrown on it.

Her eyes are shallower, as though
  Some grey glass were behind; her brow
And cheeks the straining bones show through,
  Are not so good for kissing now.

Her lips are drier now she is
  A great duke's wife these many years,
They will not shudder with a kiss
  As once they did, being moist with tears.

Also her hands have lost that way
  Of clinging that they used to have;
They look'd quite easy, as they lay
  Upon the silken cushions brave

With broidery of the apples green
  My Lord Duke bears upon his shield.
Her face, alas! that I have seen
  Look fresher than an April field,

This is all gone now; gone also
  Her tender walking; when she walks
She is most queenly I well know,
  And she is fair still:—as the stalks

Of faded summer-lilies are,
  So is she grown now unto me
This spring-time, when the flowers star
  The meadows, birds sing wonderfully.

I warrant once she used to cling
  About his neck, and kiss'd him so,
And then his coming step would ring
  Joy-bells for her,—some time ago.

Ah! sometimes like an idle dream
  That hinders true life overmuch,
Sometimes like a lost heaven, these seem—
  This love is not so hard to smutch.

ISAAC CLASON (1796?–1830)

The son of a New York merchant, Isaac Clason inherited a fortune which he spent on actresses in London and Paris, and blew all the money he could cadge from his relatives besides. He was found dead in an obscure London lodging-house. "His fate," remarks the Reverend Rufus W. Griswold in *The Poets and Poetry of America* (Philadelphia, 1845), "is an unfavourable commentary on his character." Clason's principal works appeared in 1825: two more Cantos continuing Byron's *Don Juan.*

FROM *Don Juan,* Canto XVII

He who has seen the wild tornado sweep
  (Its path destruction, and its progress death)
The silent bosom of the smiling deep
  With the black besom of its boisterous breath,
Waking to strife the slumbering waves, that leap
  In battling surges from their beds beneath,
Yawning and swelling from their liquid caves,
Like buried giants from their restless graves:—

He who has gazed on sights and scenes like these,
  Hath look'd on nature in her maddest mood;
But nature's warfare passes by degrees,—
  The thunder's voice is hush'd, however rude,
The dying winds unclasp the raging seas,
  The scowling sky throws back her cloud-capt hood,
The infant lightnings to their cradles creep,
And the gaunt earthquake rocks herself to sleep.

T. E. BROWN (1830–1897)

T. E. Brown is perhaps the supreme master of the unintentional infelicity. Henley thought Brown ought to be Poet Laureate, and he may have been right. "Here," said Henley, "is an admirable raciness, a notable pungency, a peculiar, irresistible flavor." And again, "There are moments, indeed, when that odd confession of his: 'I am a born sobber': recurs to the mind with an insistence that is not wholly agreeable. . . . I believe that, in his heart of hearts, he was not averse from 'wallowing naked in the pathetic' . . ." And of Brown's poems in Manx dialect: "He thought they would nourish and enkindle and bring on the great Manx poet. . . . What is certain is that if the great Manx poet ever comes along, here is as rare and fortifying a compost for him to nuzzle his genius in as poet ever had."

When Love Meets Love

When love meets love, breast urged to breast,
God interposes,
An unacknowledged guest,
And leaves a little child among our roses.

O, gentle hap!
O, sacred lap!
O, brooding dove!
But when he grows
Himself to be a rose,
God takes him—where is then our love?
O, where is all our love?

Between Our Folding Lips

Between our folding lips
God slips
An embryon life, and goes;
And this becomes your rose.
We love, God makes: in our sweet mirth
God spies occasion for a birth.
Then is it His, or is it ours?
I know not—He is fond of flowers.

V

Food and Drink

. . . And dote on Mother's gray and leaning head
Whenever I eat lard-and-pepper bread.
—Hanscom Wills
"Lard-and-pepper Bread"

Take him to his mother,
She'll bless you I know,
Tho' 'twas only a drunkard that fell on the snow.
—Anonymous ballad

JAMES McINTYRE (1827–1906)

In grandiose ineptitude, Canada's closest rival to McGonagall may well be McIntyre, who earned the epithet "The Cheese Poet" for this rhapsody to a four-ton prize cheese, displayed in Toronto, circa 1855. (Text cribbed from William Cole's *Fireside Book of Humorous Poetry*.)

Queen of Cheese

We have seen thee, queen of cheese,
Lying quietly at your ease,
Gently fanned by evening breeze,
Thy fair form no flies dare seize.

All gaily dressed soon you'll go
To the great Provincial show,
To be admired by many a beau
In the city of Toronto.

Cows numerous as a swarm of bees,
Or as the leaves upon the trees,
It did require to make thee please,
And stand unrivaled, queen of cheese.

May you not receive a scar as
We have heard that Mr. Harris
Intends to send you off as far as
The great world's show at Paris.

Of the youth beware of these,
For some of them might rudely squeeze
And bite your cheek, then songs or glees
We could not sing. Oh! queen of cheese

Wert thou suspended from a balloon,
You'd cast a shade even at noon,
Folks would think it was the moon
About to fall and crush them soon.

T. E. BROWN (1830–1897)

FROM Lynton Verses

Milk! milk! milk!
  Straight as the Parson's bands,
Streaming like silk
  Under and over her hands—
    What is Mary scheming?
    What is Mary dreaming?

Swish! swish! swish!
  Pressing her sweet young brow,
Smooth as a dish,
  To the side of the sober cow—
    Can she tell no tale then?
    Nought but milk and pail then?

Strip! strip! strip!
  Far away over the sea
Comes there a ship,
  The ship of all ships that be?
    Ah, little fairy!
    Ah, Mary, Mary!

BRUCE WESTON MUNRO (fl. 1893)

"A little more regard for future reputation and a little less queasy compunction about destroying the wishy-washy effusions of boyhood would no doubt have prompted the cutting out of the bulk of the book," confides Munro in his preface to *Groans and Grins of One Who Survived* (Washington, D.C., 1893). "The unkind reader may be just peevish enough to judge it by some of its dreariest tales in verse." Here is one of them.

Grandmother's Apple Pies

Deliver us from apple pies
  Made in the careless, slipshod way
Of foreign "help," who melodize
  The atmosphere with roundelay
The while they slice up skin and core,
  With apple stems and other stuff,
With fungous growth and seeds galore
  Thrown in, and crust supremely tough.

These have degraded apple pies,
  Which, though they may seem good, will straight
Rebellious stomachs agonize.
  Full of this thought, man mourns his fate,
And vows from modern pies to fast;
  I sometimes yet am fain to cry
For opportunities now past,
  When I might have refused such pie.

My grandmother made apple pies
  That every one was sure to call
A gastronomical surprise;
  For they were never known to pall
Upon the appetite. You knew,
  Beyond all doubt, if you but saw
Her *modus operandi* through,
  Her pies would be without a flaw.

In early June she used green fruit
  Till harvest apples had a chance
To ripen; and should robins loot
  Her cherries, her long gun would glance
That way, and some fine birds would die.
  Her cherry pies deserved all praise,
But her best "holt" was apple pie—
  Her specialty, in modern phrase.

Each season had its apple pie;
  The mellow bell-flower held its own
For six long weeks, but she would try
  Each apple in the temp'rate zone.
When her good pies were served with cream,
  A choice was hard; but Northern Spies
She favored most. Strange though it seem,
  Grandmother seldom ate her pies.

At Christmas-time she made mince pies
  That were delicious, though she took
Less art with them, and did not prize
  Our compliments—if we forsook
Too long her apple pies for mince,
  For turkey or for good roast beef,
Plum pudding, pumpkin pie, or quince;
  For such neglect moved her to grief.

The New Year's leaf was always turned
  With apple pie at morn and noon,
And when the springtime months returned,
  Dried apples filled the gap till June.
Those apple pies went all too fast;
  I sometimes yet am fain to cry
For opportunities now past,
  When I might have devoured more pie.

HARRY EDWARD MILLS (fl. 1901)

Punkin Pie

Say, Billie, when yer startin' off a-nuttin' with yer sack,
An' know yer goin' to git to feelin' holler 'fore yer back,
An' see yer mother puttin' up a lunch fer by an' by,
Why is it nothin' strikes you like the hunk o' punkin pie?

An' while yer huntin' fer the nuts, er somethin' you hev lost,
An' wishin' all the skeeters had got froze up with the frost,
It's funny how the crickets an' the birds an' squirrels try
To chirp an' sing an' chatter all the time 'bout punkin pie.

An' when you git to eatin', if you do the way you should,
An' tackle bread an' butter first and things that ain't so good,
What makes you jest ez hungry yit, an' pretty near ez dry
Until you git to workin' on yer piece o' punkin pie?

An' when yer done with dinner an' yer punkin pie's all et,
An' you can't help a-wishin' that you hadn't started yet;
O, ain't it nice to lick yer lips to scare away a fly,
An' find a lot remainin' from that piece o' punkin pie.

Say, Billie, I've been thinkin' when I git to be a man,
I'll hev 'bout forty acres just fer punkins ef I can.
An' maybe I'll git married, but the girl thet takes
  my eye
Must be a bird at bakin' when it comes to punkin pie.

EDWARD JOHNSON (fl. 19th century)

This British comment takes a negative view of the demon sauce; and may recall the Pharisee's prayer, "O Lord, I thank Thee that I am not as other men."

The Water-drinker

Oh! water for me! Bright water for me!
And wine for the tremulous debauchee!
It cooleth the brow, it cooleth the brain,
It maketh the faint one strong again;
It comes o'er the sense like a breeze from the sea,
All freshness, like infant purity.
Oh! water, bright water for me, for me!
Give wine, give wine to the debauchee!

Fill to the brim! Fill, fill to the brim!
Let the flowing crystal kiss the rim!
For my hand is steady, my eye is true,
For I, like the flowers, drink nought but dew.
Oh! water, bright water's a mine of wealth,
And the ores it yieldeth are vigour and health.
So water, pure water for me, for me!
And wine for the tremulous debauchee!

Fill again to the brim! again to the brim!
For water strengtheneth life and limb!
To the days of the aged it addeth length,
To the might of the strong it addeth strength.
It freshens the heart, it brightens the sight,
'Tis like quaffing a goblet of morning light!

So, Water! I will drink nought but thee,
Thou parent of health and energy!

When o'er the hills, like a gladsome bride,
Morning walks forth in her beauty's pride,
And, leading a band of laughing hours,
Brushes the dew from the nodding flowers;
Oh! cheerily then my voice is heard,
Mingling with that of the soaring bird,
Who flingeth abroad his matins loud,
As he freshens his wing in the cold gray cloud.

But when Evening has quitted her sheltering yew,
Drowsily flying and weaving anew
Her dusky meshes o'er land and sea—
How gently, O sleep! fall thy poppies on me;
For I drink water, pure, cold, and bright,
And my dreams are of heaven the livelong night;
So, hurrah! for thee, Water! hurrah, hurrah!
Thou art silver and gold, thou art riband and star!
Hurrah! for bright Water! hurrah, hurrah!

VI

Nature

O'er ten thousand, thousand acres,
  Goes light the nimble zephyr;
The Flowers—tiny sect of Shakers—
  Worship him ever.

—Ralph Waldo Emerson,
"To Ellen at the South"

He viewed the uncovered bottom of the abyss . . .

—John Dyer,
"The Fleece"

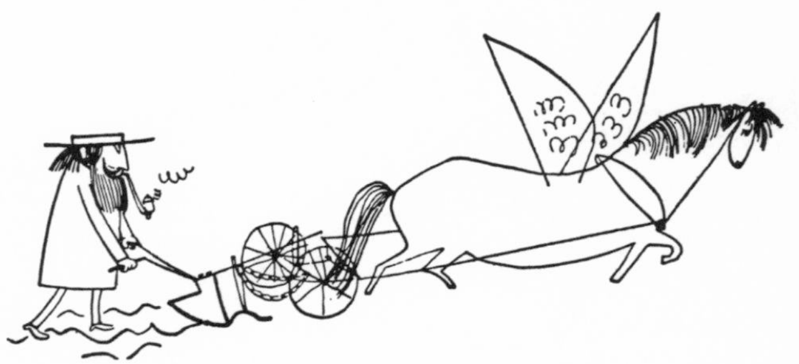

HARRY EDWARD MILLS (fl. 1901)

The Early Frogs

O, I love to hear the frogs
  When they first begin to sing;
How they vocalize the bogs,
  And vociferate the Spring.
How they carol as they croak,
  How they mingle jest and joke
With their solemn chant and dirge
  On the river's slimy verge.

O, I love to hear the frogs,
  For their monotone uncouth
Is the music of the cogs
  Of the mill wheel of my youth.
And I listen half asleep,
  And the eyes of mem'ry peep
Through the bars that hold me fast,
  From the pleasures of the past.

O, I love to hear the frogs,
  For their melody is health
To the heart that worry flogs
  With the lash of want or wealth.
And the cares of life take wing,
  And its pleasures lose their sting,
And love's channel way unclogs
  In the croaking of the frogs.

ELLA WHEELER WILCOX (1850–1919)

Attraction

The meadow and the mountain with desire
  Gazed on each other, till a fierce unrest
  Surged 'neath the meadow's seemingly calm breast,
And all the mountain's fissures ran with fire.

A mighty river rolled between them there.
  What could the mountain do but gaze and burn?
  What could the meadow do but look and yearn,
And gem its bosom to conceal despair?

Their seething passion agitated space,
  Till lo! the lands a sudden earthquake shook,
  The river fled: the meadow leaped, and took
The leaning mountain in a close embrace.

T. E. BROWN (1830–1897)

My Garden

A garden is a lovesome thing, God wot!
Rose plot,
Fringed pool,
Ferned grot—
The veriest school
Of peace; and yet the fool
Contends that God is not—
Not God! in gardens! when the eve is cool?
Nay, but I have a sign;
'Tis very sure God walks in mine.

I Bended Unto Me

I bended unto me a bough of May,
That I might see and smell:
It bore it in a sort of way,
It bore it very well.
But, when I let it backward sway,
Then it were hard to tell
With what a toss, with what a swing,
The dainty thing
Resumed its proper level,
And sent me to the devil.
I know it did—you doubt it?
I turned, and saw them whispering about it.

ANONYMOUS (fl. 1837)

From an old newspaper, the Salisbury (North Carolina) *Carolina Watchman*, Richard Walser excavated this frank confession for his anthology *Nematodes in My Garden of Verse*.

'Another sin I had forgot'

Another sin I had forgot:
That hog I killed in my back lot.
I aimed the brickbat at his head;
When I went up I found it dead.
I quickly drew him to the gate
And there a while on him did wait.
I tried to get him to stand up,
But found with him the jigg was up.
I told the neighbors all along

That he got foundered there on corn;
But now they have it sung about,
I killed him there and threw him out.

RALPH WALDO EMERSON (1803–1882)

Miss Elisabeth Luther Cary once wrote that however diligently we may search for flaws in the poetry of Emerson, "we shall not have disturbed by a hair's breadth our inner knowledge that we have been pecking and quibbling over the loveliest product of our national life." Those who would persevere in pecking about so unpatriotically, however, might bring to bear a critical principle once articulated by Emerson himself while rejecting, ever so tactfully, some verses submitted to the *Dial* by one Miss Woodbridge: "In short, all poetry should be original & necessary."

FROM Excelsior

Over his head were the maple buds,
And over the tree was the moon,
And over the moon were the starry studs
That drop from the angels' shoon.

ANONYMOUS

In his epic *Thalaba the Destroyer*, Robert Southey glosses his own line,

She stared me in the face—

by quoting his source, "one of the most beautiful passages of our old ballads, so full of beauty." This ballad should perhaps not be held against The Folk, since Southey admits to having "with some trouble . . . procured only an imperfect copy from memory."

Old Poulter's Mare

At length old age came on her,
  And she grew faint and poor;
Her master he fell out with her,
  And turn'd her out of door,
Saying, if thou wilt not labor,
  I prithee go thy way,—
And never let me see thy face
  Until thy dying day.

These words she took unkind,
  And on her way she went,
For to fulfil her master's will
  Always was her intent;
The hills were very high,
  The valleys very bare,
The summer it was hot and dry,—
  It starved Old Poulter's Mare.

Old Poulter he grew sorrowful,
  And said to his kinsman Will,
I'd have thee go and seek the Mare
  O'er valley and o'er hill;
Go, go, go, go says Poulter,
  And make haste back again,
For until thou hast found the Mare,
  In grief I shall remain.

Away went Will so willingly,
  And all day long he sought;
Till when it grew towards the night,
  He in his mind bethought,

He would go home and rest him,
  And come again to-morrow;
For if he could not find the Mare,
  His heart would break with sorrow

He went a little further,
  And turn'd his head aside,
And just by goodman Whitfield's gate,
  Oh, there the Mare he spied.
He ask her how she did;
  She stared him in the face,
Then down she laid her head again—
  She was in wretched case.

MARTIN FARQUHAR TUPPER (1810–1889)

Karl Marx used to play with his daughters a game called "Confessions," where they asked him very personal questions and he supplied the answers. Some of these exchanges have been preserved:

Your favorite virtue—Simplicity.
Your chief characteristic—Singleness of purpose.
Your idea of happiness—To fight.
Your idea of misery—Submission.
The vice you detest most—Servility.
Your pet aversion—Martin Tupper.

Tupper was best known for *Proverbial Philosophy*, four volumes of profound moral suggestions in flabby free verse that make one think of a somewhat more worldly Kahlil Gibran. He was however, a rhymster as well, as our selection proves.

Mercy to Animals

A BALLAD OF HUMANITY.

O boys and men of British mould,
  With mother's milk within you!
A simple word for young and old,
  A word to warm and win you;
You've each and all got human hearts
  As well as human features,
So hear me, while I take the parts
  Of all the poor dumb creatures.

I wot your lot is sometimes rough;
  But theirs is something rougher,—
No hopes, no loves,—but pain enough,
  And only sense to suffer:
You, men and boys, have friends and joys,
  And homes, and hopes in measure,—
But these poor brutes are only mutes,
  And never knew a pleasure!

A little water, chaff and hay,
  And sleep, the boon of Heaven,
How great returns for these have they
  To your advantage given:
And yet the worn-out horse, or ass,
  Who makes your daily gaining,
Is paid with goad and thong, alas!
  Though nobly uncomplaining.

Stop, cruel boy! you mean no ill,
  But never thought about it,—
Why beat that patient donkey still?
  He goes as well without it:
Here, taste and try a cut or two,—
  Ha! you can shout and feel it;

Boy—that was Mercy's hint to you,—
  In shorter measure deal it.

Stop, sullen man! 'tis true to tell
  How ill the world has used you;
The farmers didn't treat you well,
  The squire's self refused you:
But is that any reason why
  A bad revenge you're wreaking
On that poor lame old horse,—whose eye
  Rebukes you without speaking?

O think not thou that this dumb brute
  Has no strong Friend to aid him;
Nor hope, because his wrongs are mute,
  They rouse not GOD who made him!
A little while, and you are—dead,
  With all your bitter feelings;
How will the Judge, so just and dread,
  Reward your cruel dealings?

Go, do some good before you die
  To those who make your living;
They will not ask you reasons why,
  Nor tax you for forgiving:
Their mouths are mute; but most acute
  The woes whereby you wear them;
Then come with me, and only see
  How easy 'tis to spare them!

Load for'ard; neither goad, nor flog;
  For *rest* your beast is flagging:
And do not let that willing dog
  Tear out his heart with dragging:
Wait, wait awhile; those axles grease,
  And shift this buckle's fretting;
And give that galling collar ease;—
  How grateful is he getting!

So poor yourselves, and short of joys,
  Unkindly used, unfairly,
I sometimes wonder, men and boys,
  You're merciful so rarely:
If you have felt how hunger gripes,
  Why famish and ill use 'em?
If you've been weal'd by sores and stripes,
  How can you beat and bruise 'em?

O, fear! lest GOD has taught in vain,
  And so your hearts you harden;
Oh, hope! for lo! He calls again,
  And *now*'s the time for pardon:
Yes, haste to-day to put away
  Your cruelties and curses,—
And man at least, if not his beast,
  Shall bless me for my verses.

WILLIAM DIAPER (1685–1717)

Trying to reconstruct the character of William Diaper, Geoffrey Grigson supposed it marked by "swagger, bounce, obsequiousness, spinelessness, perhaps a smartness and snottiness." Diaper is referred to, also, in Swift's *Journal to Stella.* ("His name is Diaper," says Swift, "P—— on him.") Such piddling comment hardly does justice to a poet who invented nothing less than a whole new genre of literature: the underwater pastoral. Although in his *Piscatorie Eclogs* (1633), Phineas Fletcher had tried unsuccessfully to jive up the pastoral tradition by substituting fisherfolk for sheep-tenders, it remained for Diaper to submerge pastoral poetry all the way. His *Nereides, or Sea-Ecologues* (1712) replace the nymphs and swains of Theocritus by nereids and mermen; sheep by dogfish; grain by seaweed. Pope was skeptical in *The Dunciad*:

Far worse unhappy D——r succeeds,
He searched for coral, but he gather'd weeds.

In fact, after Diaper, the genre has had no known practitioners.

FROM Eclogue I

Glaucus: Believe not, Fair, that I can prove untrue,
Or any Water-Beauty love, but you.
No, first the Waves shall lose their biting Salts,
The Winds shall cease to sound in hollow Vaults,
And wanton Fish shall leave their native Seas,
And bask on Earth, or brouse on leavy Trees.

FREDERICK LOCKER-LAMPSON (1821–1895)

Frederick Locker, who took the name Lampson after his second marriage, a union that made him financially independent and therefore able to ride his Pegasus on unobstructed courses, wrote only one book of verse: the best-selling *London Lyrics*. "True they are colorless," wrote William Henley of Lampson's poems, "but they are so luminously limpid and serene, they are so sprightly and graceful and gay . . . how clean the English."

A Garden Lyric

(GERALDINE AND I)

Di te, Damasippe, deaeque
Verum ob consilium donent tonsore.

We have loiter'd and laugh'd in the flowery croft,
  We have met under wintry skies;
Her voice is the dearest voice, and soft
  Is the light in her wistful eyes;
It is bliss in the silent woods, among
  Gay crowds, or in any place,
To mould her mind, to gaze in her young
          Confiding face.

For ever may roses divinely blow,
  And wine-dark pansies charm
By that prim box path where I felt the glow,
  Of her dimpled, trusting arm,
And the sweep of her silk as she turn'd and smiled
  A smile as pure as her pearls;
The breeze was in love with the darling Child,
          And coax'd her curls.

She show'd me her ferns and woodbine sprays,
  Foxglove and jasmine stars,
A mist of blue in the beds, a blaze
  Of red in the celadon jars:
And velvety bees in convolvulus bells,
  And roses of bountiful Spring.
But I said—"Though roses and bees have spells,
          They have thorn, and sting."

She show'd me ripe peaches behind a net
  As fine as her veil, and fat
Goldfish a-gape, who lazily met
  For her crumbs—I grudged them that!

A squirrel, some rabbits with long lop ears,
And guinea-pigs, tortoise-shell—wee;
And I told her that eloquent truth inheres
In all we see.

I lifted her doe by its lops, quoth I,
"Even here deep meaning lies,—
Why have squirrels these ample tails, and why
Have rabbits these prominent eyes?"
She smiled and said, as she twirl'd her veil,
"For some nice little cause, no doubt—
If you lift a guinea-pig by the tail
His eyes drop out!"

T. E. BROWN (1830–1897)

The Voices of Nature

This cluck of water in the tangles—
What said it to the Angles?
What to the Jutes,
This wave sip-sopping round the salt sea-roots?
With what association did it hit on
The tympanum of a Damnonian Briton?
To tender Guinevere, to Britomart,
The stout of heart,
Along the guarded beach
Spoke it the same sad speech
It speaks to me—
This sopping of the sea?

Surely the plash
Of water upon stones,
Encountering in their ears the tones

Of dominant passions masterful,
Made but a bourdon for the chord
Of a great key, that rested lord
Of all the music, straining not the bones
Of Merlin's scull;
And in the ear of Vivian its frets
Were silver castanets,
That tinkled 'mong the vanities, and quickened
The free, full-blooded pulse,
Nor sickened
Her soul, nor stabbed her to the heart.
Strange! that to me this gurgling of the dulse
Allays no smart,
Consoles no nerve,
Rounds off no curve—
Alack!
Comes rather like a sigh,
A question that has no reply—
Opens a deep misgiving
What is this life I'm living—
Our fathers were not so—
Silence, thou moaning wrack!
And yet . . . I do not know.
And yet . . . I would go back.

X. J. KENNEDY (b. 1929)

At the age of 16 Kennedy edited a mimeographed periodical called *Vampire*. In four years' time in the United States Navy he attained the rating of Journalist Second Class; then spent six years in Ann Arbor, Michigan, failing to complete a doctorate.

FROM An unfinished work

Nature might chicken out, but "I love you"
He said and meant it, wrestling down to earth
Her flesh. She stared at him with skies so blue
His heart lay down, took ether, and gave birth.

SYDNEY DOBELL (1824–1874)

Wind

Oh the wold, the wold,
Oh the wold, the wold!
Oh the winter stark,
Oh the level dark,
On the wold, the wold, the wold!

Oh the wold, the wold,
Oh the wold, the wold!
Oh the mystery
Of the blasted tree
On the wold, the wold, the wold!

Oh the wold, the wold,
Oh the wold, the wold!
Oh the owlet's croon
To the haggard moon,
To the waning moon,
On the wold, the wold, the wold!

Oh the wold, the wold,
Oh the wold, the wold!
Oh the fleshless stare,

Oh the windy hair,
On the wold, the wold, the wold!

Oh the wold, the wold,
Oh the wold, the wold!
Oh the cold sigh,
Oh the hollow cry,
The lean and hollow cry,
On the wold, the wold, the wold!

Oh the wold, the wold,
Oh the wold, the wold!
Oh the white sight,
Oh the shuddering night,
The shivering shuddering night,
On the wold, the wold, the wold!

THOMAS HOLLEY CHIVERS (1809–1858)

Chivers is, according to S. Foster Damon in a generally sympathetic study, "the supreme example of genius wholly unregulated by any talent whatever." Controversy over whether Chivers plagiarized from Poe or Poe from Chivers has kept Chivers from being read, or even printed. Only one side of his genius—a surprisingly well developed taste for abstract sound patterns that impressed not only Poe but Swinburne and Rossetti—is evident in the following excerpt, but only slightly.

FROM Chinese Serenade for the Ut-Kam and Tong-Koo

Tu Du,
Skies blue—

All clear—
Fourth year,
Third moon,
High noon
At night;
And the stars shine bright . . .

VII

War, Patriotism, and Local Pride

Mannahatta a-march—and it's O to sing it well!
It's O for a manly life in the camp.
—W. Whitman,
"Drum Taps"

Scourge us as Thou wilt, oh Lord God of Hosts;
Deal with us, Lord, according to our transgressions;
But give us Victory!
Victory, victory! oh, Lord, victory!
Oh, Lord, victory! Lord, Lord, Victory!
—Sydney Dobell,
"In War-Time, a Psalm of the Heart"

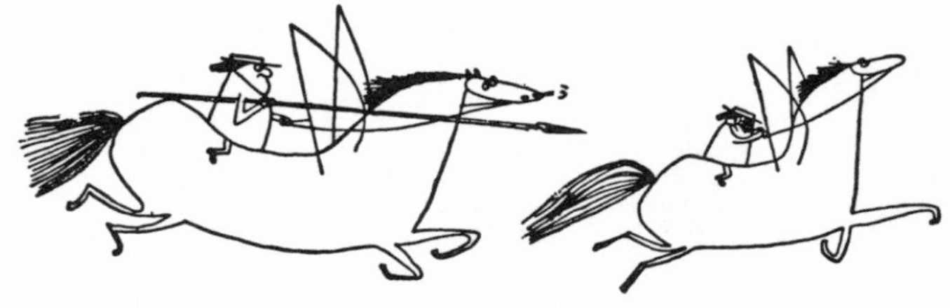

JULIA A. MOORE (1847–1920)

It is difficult to realize that the Sweet Singer of Michigan, undoubtedly the most celebrated bad poet America has produced, lived long enough to be a contemporary of Lawrence Ferlinghetti. That Mrs. Moore recalls an earlier, less conscious age, may be because her whole output of poetry was published in Grand Rapids between 1876 and 1878 (in two collections, *The Sentimental Song Book* and *A Few Choice Words to the Public*). She seems then to have abandoned poetry at the insistence of her husband, and taken up novel writing. Well may Mr. Moore have feared for her life. At one public reading, an unsympathetic audience drew her to bark: "You think you paid twenty cents to look at a fool, well, who's the more fool? I have your twenty cents."

Eminent among her cult of mock admirers was Mark Twain, who in *Huckleberry Finn* may have taken her maudlin elegies to dead infants as models for the work of Emmeline Grangerford. More lately, Ogden Nash has acknowledged his debt to her. Certainly few poets have so assiduously cultivated the line that rambles on for as long as necessary, nor produced more surprising rimes. Given the first three lines of this quatrain, who could predict the way the fourth would end?

Many a man joined a club
  That never drank a dram,
Those noble men were kind and brave,
  They do not care ——.

Could Pope himself have finished that line more unexpectedly? It goes, "They do not care for slang." As the anonymous editor of a 1912 reprint edition of *The Sentimental Song Book* has remarked, Mrs. Moore "not only conveys information, but she brings the mind up with a jerk. We look around quickly to see what made the noise, and feel instinctively for our money and our watch."

FROM Grand Rapids Cricket Club

Brave Kelso, he's considered great,
  Chief of the club he is found;
Great crowds he draws to see him bowl
  The ball upon the ground.
And Mr. Follet is very brave,
  A lighter player than the rest,
He got struck severe at the fair ground
  For which he took a rest.

ELLA WHEELER WILCOX (1850–1919)

The True Knight

We sigh above historic pages,
  Brave with the deeds of courtly men,
And wish those peers of middle ages
  In our dull day could live again.
And yet no knight or troubadour began
In chivalry with the American.

He does not frequent joust or tourney
  And flaunt his lady's colours there;
But in the tedium of a journey,
  He shows that deferential care—
That thoughtful kindness to the sex at large,
Which makes each woman feel herself his charge.

He does not challenge foes to duel,
  To win his lady's cast-off glove,
But proves in ways less rash and cruel,
  The truth and fervour of his love.
Not by bold deeds, but by his reverent mien,
He pays his public tribute to his Queen.

He may not shine with courtly graces,
  But yet, his kind, respectful air
To woman, whatsoe'er her place is,
  It might be well if kings could share.
So, for the chivalric true gentleman,
Give me, I say, our own American.

ROBERT BROWNING (1812–1889)

The action of Browning's poem takes place in the Metidja Desert in Algeria; the speaker is an Arab soldier galloping hell-for-leather to the side of his general, Abd-el-Kadr. At the moment, the Arabs are carving up the French army; and the speaker has a vision of enemy corpses beneath the sliding sands. It may be that the motion of his horse inspires him (in stanza one) with a keener perception of the Prophet's message. It may be, however, that the whole thing means nothing like that at all.

Through the Metidja to Abd-el-Kadr

As I ride, as I ride,
With a full heart for my guide,
So its tide rocks my side,
As I ride, as I ride.
That, as I were double-eyed,

He, in whom our Tribes confide,
Is discried, ways untried,
As I ride, as I ride.

As I ride, as I ride
To our Chief and his Allied,
Who dares chide my heart's pride
As I ride, as I ride?
Or are witnesses denied—
Through the desert waste and wide
Do I glide unespied
As I ride, as I ride?

As I ride, as I ride,
When an inner voice has cried,
The sands slide, nor abide
(As I ride, as I ride)
O'er each visioned homicide
That came vaunting (has he lied?)
To reside—where he died,
As I ride, as I ride.

As I ride, as I ride,
Ne'er has spur my swift horse plied,
Yet his hide, streaked and pied,
As I ride, as I ride,
Shows where sweat has sprung and dried
Zebra-footed, ostrich-thighed—
How has vied stride with stride
As I ride, as I ride!

As I ride, as I ride,
Could I loose what Fate has tied,
Ere I pried, she should hide
(As I ride, as I ride)
All that's meant me—satisfied
When the Prophet and the Bride

Stop veins I'd have subside
As I ride, as I ride!

GEORGE HENRY BOKER (1823–1890)

Poet, professor, and diplomat, Boker is remembered mainly as a none-too-successful imitator of Shakespeare. His Civil War poem, "Dirge for a Soldier," was anthologized by Whittier, who praised it as one of the greatest threnodies ever penned. A curious production of Boker's blank verse tragedy, *Francesca da Rimini*, was staged at the University of Michigan in 1959, slightly done over into beat diction and retitled, *The Quivering Aardvark and the Jelly of Love*. A comparative statistical analysis of the syntax of Shakespeare and Boker has been made by the critic Mel Wolf, who concludes that as playwrights the two developed pretty much along the same lines; statistically, that is.

Dirge for a Soldier

Close his eyes; his work is done!
What to him is friend or foeman,
Rise of moon, or set of sun,
Hand of man, or kiss of woman?
Lay him low, lay him low,
In the clover or the snow!
What cares he? he cannot know:
Lay him low!

As man may, he fought his fight,
Proved his truth by his endeavor;
Let him sleep in solemn night,
Sleep forever and forever.

Lay him low, lay him low,
In the clover or the snow!
What cares he? he cannot know:
Lay him low!

Fold him in his country's stars,
Roll the drum and fire the volley!
What to him are all our wars,
What but death-bemocking folly?
Lay him low, lay him low,
In the clover or the snow!
What cares he? he cannot know:
Lay him low!

Leave him to God's watching eye,
Trust him to the hand that made him.
Mortal love weeps idly by:
God alone has power to aid him.
Lay him low, lay him low,
In the clover or the snow!
What cares he? he cannot know:
Lay him low!

JOSEPH SHIPPEY, A.B. (fl. 1810)

All that is known about Joseph Shippey is that he was graduated from Columbia College in 1796, and lived to tell the tale.

Columbia College, 1796

Columbia College! Alma Mater! well
Do I remember, and the time could tell,
When first escaped from pedagogic rule,

To thee I came fresh from a grammar school
From five long years well stored, at all events,
With English, Greek, and Latin rudiments.
And how I profited, thy books can show:
Placed number four, with twenty-eight below.

JOSEPH SAMUEL REED (fl. 1914–1918)

Of the author of "A Soldier's Plea for the Y.M.C.A." nothing is known, except that his daughter played the harp.

A Soldier's Plea for the Y.M.C.A.

Praise be to those who gave it birth—
True Guardian Angel here on Earth—
  As constant as a Mother;
A refuge when Temptation's strong
To be enticed by a Siren's song,
  As of't befalls a brother.

The virons of the Soldier's "Y"
On which all Mothers can rely—
  Is on a broad plane truly—
No matter what one's faith or creed,
  His spiritual or temporal need,
  Is minister to, and duly.

The Y is truly the Soldier's Home,
Here he may find his fav'rite tome,
  And here puruse its pages;
Tis here, he to the Home-folks writes
Tells of his worries and delights
  As Knights in by-gone Ages.

'Tis heart some learn our language too—
As all good foreigners should do—
  And Fraternize together;
Here many a wholsome jest and quip,
Enjoying sweet Companionship,
  Despite the stormy weather.

Here best of Movie films unroll
To please the eye, and feast the soul—
  May we embrace it ever?
At Chapel service, free from strife,
Is offered us the Bread of Life
  To strengthen our endeavor.

When those on you for money call,
Remember we have given our all
  E'en to our life's blood flowing—
So, make your contributions strong,
To help this great adjunct along
  For it must be kept going.

BRET HARTE (1836–1902)

It is said that when Bret Harte made his first trip East, his train was mobbed at several stops and he was treated in much the same way a movie star is treated in our own era. This intense fame died quickly, but, curiously enough, though critics and other well-wishers have pronounced his death many times, he has a strange way of lingering on in anthologies and even in movie adaptations.

What the Bullet Sang

O joy of creation
To be!
O rapture to fly
And be free!
Be the battle lost or won,
Though its smoke shall hide the sun,
I shall find my love,—the one
Born for me!

I shall know him where he stands,
All alone,
With the power in his hands
Not o'erthrown;
I shall know him by his face,
By his godlike front and grace;
I shall hold him for a space,
All my own!

It is he—O my love!
So bold!
It is I—all thy love
Foretold!
It is I. O love! what bliss!
Dost thou answer to my kiss?
O sweetheart! what is this
Lieth there so cold?

ANONYMOUS (1745)

The following poem was first printed in *Harmonia Anglicana; The Gentleman's Magazine.*

God Save the King

God save Great *George* our King,
Long live our noble King,
  God save the King.
Send him Victorious,
Happy and Glorious,
Long to reign over us,
  God save the King.

O Lord our God arise,
Scatter his Enemies,
  And make them fall:
Confound their Politicks,
Frustrate their Knavish Tricks,
On him our Hopes we fix,
  God save us all.

Thy choicest Gifts in Store,
On him be pleas'd to pour,
  Long may he reign.
May he defend our Laws,
And ever give us Cause,
To sing with Heart and Voice
  God save the King.

Lord grant that Marshal *Wade*
May by thy Mighty Aid
  Victory bring.
May he Sedition hush,
And like a Torrent rush,
Rebellious Scots to crush,
  God save the King.

WILLIAM COWPER (1731–1800)

Much of Cowper's life was spent in studying law, translating Homer, breeding rabbits, and lolling in melancholy.

FROM On the Queen's Visit to London, The Night of the Seventeenth of March, 1789

When, long sequester'd from his throne,
  George took his seat again,
By right of worth, not blood alone,
  Entitled here to reign.

Then loyalty, with all his lamps
  New trimm'd, a gallant show!
Chasing the darkness and the damps,
  Set London in a glow.

'Twas hard to tell, of streets or squares,
  Which form'd the chief display,
These most resembling cluster'd stars,
  Those the long milky way.

Bright shone the roofs, the domes, the spires,
  And rockets flew, self-driven,
To hang their momentary fires
  Amid the vault of heaven.

So fire with water to compare,
  The ocean serves, on high
Up-spouted by a whale in air,
  To express unwieldy joy.

Had all the pageants of the world
  In one procession join'd,

And all the banners been unfurl'd
  That heralds e'er design'd,

For no such sight had England's Queen
  Forsaken her retreat,
Where George, recover'd, made a scene
  Sweet always, doubly sweet.

HERMAN MELVILLE (1819–1891)

In 1859 Melville's wife wrote to her mother, "Herman has taken to writing poetry. You need not tell anyone, for you know how such things get around." And indeed he had. Melville wrote enough poetry of genuine merit between the 1850s and his death to make him probably the third best American poet of the nineteenth century. Most of the poetry that was at first dismissed as pastiche or unintentionally crude is now accepted on its own terms. However, it is in his poetry about the Civil War that we find infelicity triumphant. While "Lyon, the Battle of Springfield" does not wing its way to the depths discovered by George Henry Boker's patriotic lamentations, it does give us a remarkable example of the poet encircled by his own strategy, riding furiously through a fusillade of bad rhymes, rocking horse meters and bellicose images, arriving slain at the very portal of victory, triumphantly beating a dead horse.

Lyon

BATTLE OF SPRINGFIELD, MISSOURI (AUGUST, 1861)

Some hearts there are of deeper sort,
    Prophetic, sad,

Which yet for cause are trebly clad;
Known death they fly on:
This wizard-heart and heart-of-oak had Lyon.

"They are more than twenty thousand strong,
We less than five,
Too few with such a host to strive."
"Such counsel, fie on!
'Tis battle, or 'tis shame;" and firm stood Lyon.

"For help at need in vain we wait—
Retreat or fight:
Retreat the foe would take for flight,
And each proud scion
Feel more elate; the end must come," said Lyon.

By candlelight he wrote the will,
And left his all
To Her for whom 'twas not enough to fall;
Loud neighed Orion
Without the tent; drums beat; we marched with
Lyon.

The night-tramp done, we spied the Vale
With guard-fires lit;
Day broke, but trooping clouds made gloom of it:
"A field to die on,"
Presaged, in his unfaltering heart, brave Lyon.

We fought on the grass, we bled in the corn—
Fate seemed malign;
His horse the Leader led along the line—
Star-browed Orion;
Bitterly fearless, he rallied us there, brave Lyon.

There came a sound like the slitting of air
By a swift sharp sword—

A rush of the sound; and the sleek chest broad
Of black Orion
Heaved, and was fixed; the dead mane waved toward
Lyon.

"General, you're hurt—this sleet of balls!"
He seemed half spent;
With moody and bloody brow, he lowly bent:
"The field to die on;
But not—not yet; the day is long," breathed Lyon.

For a time becharmed there fell a lull
In the heart of the fight;
The tree-tops nod, the slain sleep light;
Warm noon-winds sigh on,
And thoughts which he never spake had Lyon.

Texans and Indians trim for a charge:
"Stand ready, men!
Let them come close, right up, and then
After the lead, the iron;
Fire, and charge back!" So strength returned to Lyon.

The Iowa men who held the van,
Half drilled, were new
To battle: "Some one lead us, then we'll do,"
Said Corporal Tryon:
"Men! *I* will lead," and a light glared in Lyon.

On they came: they yelped, and fired;
His spirit sped;
We levelled right in, and the half-breeds fled,
Nor stayed the iron,
Nor captured the crimson corse of Lyon.

This seer foresaw his soldier-doom,
Yet willed the fight.

He never turned; his only flight
Was up to Zion,
Where prophets now and armies greet pale Lyon.

WILLIAM FALCONER (1736 or '37–1769?)

Falconer was described by someone who knew him as "a lumpish, heavy-looking lad, very careless and dirty in his dress, and was known by the appellation of Bubly-hash-Falconer." All his brothers and sisters were deaf and dumb. He received practically no education and, perhaps against his will, became a sailor. In 1762 his poem in three cantos, *The Shipwreck*, was compared favorably with the *Aeneid*, but its reputation has declined. He was lost at sea, on the frigate *Aurora*.

Description of a Ninety Gun Ship

Amidst a wood of oaks with canvas leaves,
Which form'd a floating forest on the waves,
There stood a tower, whose vast stupendous size
Rear'd its huge mast, and seem'd to gore the skies,
From which a bloody pendant stretch'd afar
Its comet-tail, denouncing ample war;
Two younger giants* of inferior height
Display'd their sporting streamers to the sight:
The base below, another island rose,
To pour Britannia's thunder on her foes:
With bulk immense, like Ætna, she surveys
Above the rest, the lesser Cyclades:
Profuse of gold, in lustre like the sun,
Splendid with regal luxury she shone,
Lavish in wealth, luxuriant in her pride,

* Fore and mizzen masts. [author's note]

Behold the gilded mass exulting ride!
Her curious prow divides the silver waves,
In the salt ooze her radiant sides she laves,
From stem to stern, her wondrous length survey,
Rising a beauteous Venus from the sea;
Her stem, with naval drapery engraved,
Show'd mimic warriors, who the tempest braved;
Whose visage fierce defied the lashing surge,
Of Gallic pride the emblematic scourge.
Tremendous figures, lo! her stern displays,
And hold a pharos* of distinguish'd blaze;
By night it shines a star of brightest form,
To point her way, and light her through the storm:
See dread engagements pictured to the life,
See admirals maintain the glorious strife:
Here breathing images in painted ire,
Seem for their country's freedom to expire;
Victorious fleets the flying fleets pursue,
Here strikes a ship, and there exults a crew:
A frigate here blows up with hideous glare,
And adds fresh terrors to the bleeding war.
But leaving feigned ornaments, behold!
Eight hundred youths of heart and sinew bold,
Mount up her shrouds, or to her tops ascend,
Some haul her braces, some her foresail bend;
Full ninety brazen guns her port-holes fill,
Ready with nitrous magazines to kill,
From dread embrasures formidably peep,
And seem to threaten ruin to the deep;
On pivots fix'd, the well-ranged swivels lie,
Or to point downward, or to brave the sky;
While peteraroes swell with infant rage,
Prepared, though small, with fury to engage.
Thus arm'd, may Britain long her state maintain,
And with triumphant navies rule the main.

* Her poop lanthorn. [author's note]

VIII

Social Comment

The press restrained! nefandous thought!
—Matthew Green,
"The Spleen"

And who knows where she is today? Despised? Adrift
on the street?
And touched with a loathsome pest, and foul from
her head to her feet?
—J. W. Scholl,
"The Bastard of Old Sir Hugh's"

C. BUTLER-ANDREWS (fl. 1900)

Carry Nation, most famous of saloon-wreckers, tells in her autobiography how as a young and innocent girl she fell in love with, and married, a Dr. Gloyd. Alas, he turned out to be a drunkard. "When Dr. Gloyd came up to marry me the 21st of November, 1867, I noticed with pain, that his countenance was not bright, he was changed. . . . I did not find Dr. Gloyd the lover I expected." In the course of her long life, she seems hardly ever to have met anyone not bearing the "marks of dissipation." Nevertheless, the second edition of *The Use and Need of the Life of Carry Nation*, "Written By Herself" (1908), sold 10,000 copies and contained several poetic tributes to the "Hatchet Crusade," one by Butler-Andrews.

That Little Hatchet

A century was fading fast,
When o'er its closing decade passed
A matron's figure, chaste, yet bold,
Who held within her girdle's fold
A bran' new hatchet.

The jointists smiled within their bars,
'Mid bottles, mirrors and cigars—
The woman passed behind each screen,
And soon occurred a "literal" scene—
Rum, ruin, racket!

At first she "moral suasion" tried,
But lawless men mere "talk" deride:—

'Twas then she seized her household ax
And for enforcing law by acts,
Found nought to match it.

The work thus wrought with zeal discreet,
Has saved that town from rum complete;
Proving that woman's moral force
Like man's, is held, as last resource,
By sword or hatchet.

And following up that dauntless raid,
The nation welcomes her crusade;
All o'er the land, pure women charmed,
Are eager forming, each one armed
With glittering hatchets.

Talk of "defenders of the nation!"
Woman's slight arm sends consternation
'Mong its worst foes, on social fields,
Worse than the "Mauser," when she wields
The "smashing" hatchet.

Mohammed sought by arts refined,
To raise his standard o'er mankind;
But found success for aye denied,
Until at length he boldly tried
The battle-hatchet.

When soon his power imperial, shone
O'er countless tribes, in widening zone;
And wine was banished from the board
Of Moslem millions, by the sword
And victor's hatchet.

And men, once slaves, their freedom gained
By force, and power at length attained;

So, cultured brains and force combined,
Shall mark the sphere of womankind
And surely reach it.

In valor, more Joan d'Arc's are needed,
Woman's high social power's conceded,
But she herself, must blaze the path
To public morals, by her own worth
And "Little Hatchet."

KATIE V. HALL (fl. 1895–1937)

In the arena of pious song-writing, Katie V. Hall stands like a triumphant gladiator. A worker in the Olive Branch Mission, Chicago, from 1895 to 1928, Miss Hall wrote generously for church hymnbooks and periodicals. Some of her lustiest songs were collected in *Gems of Comfort, Praise and Victory* (Chicago, 1937). In her photographs, shown as a young woman and again as an octogenarian, Miss Hall radiates stern kindliness, impatience, and displeasure. Hatred of human frailty, it would seem, brought out the best in her.

The Old Filthy Beer Pail

How dark to my mind are the scenes of my childhood,
As sad recollections recall them to me;
Instead of the pure, running brook and the wildwood
Were rivers of sin flowing steady and free.
The theaters, shows and saloons that were handy,
The staggering men who went in them by scores,
I ne'er shall be able to blot from my mem'ry
While toiling down here upon life's weary shores.

How oft did my father and mother then send me
With pitcher or pail for the light, foaming beer;
Or else, some near neighbors would offer me pennies
To bring them a pint their low spirits to cheer(?).
Ah! thus did the devil lay traps for my footsteps,
To blight my young life ere I knew his dark plan;
And as I returned with the dirty old beer pail,
He whispered, "Now taste it, and be like a man."

How well I remember the boys on the corner,
Their cigarets rolling and lighting by turn;
Then gazing in wonder upon the vile pictures
Where more of the devil's black arts they might learn.
Then think of the swearing and lewd conversation
That blighted and poisoned my young, tender heart.
Ah! can you but weep at such awful temptations
That come to a boy or a girl in these parts?

The wide-open doors of saloons and low houses
Were waiting to greet me wherever I turned;
I saw at the bars, and at wine tables sitting,
The fallen of earth who fair purity spurned.
Ah, sad! yes, so sad is the dark recollection
Of days of my youth in this "Sodom" of sin.
Oh, blest is the child who is reared in the country,
Away from Chicago's defilement and din!

Oh! can you not help them—these sinned-against children?
Oh! should they be left to drift on with the tide?
Those innocent, angel-faced, dear little rosebuds,
'Twere better they had in their babyhood died.
Arouse ye, arouse ye, brave men of this nation!
Vote down the vile places which ruin the young!

Remove from their pathway these glaring temptations,
And then a glad victory song may be sung.

J. W. SCHOLL (fl. 1900)

Author of a long poem on Colonel Ingersoll, *The Light-Bearer of Liberty* (1899), Scholl had an interesting sense of rhyme:

> Gooing babies, helpless pygmies,
> Who shall solve your Fate's enigmas?

Our selection is from another volume, *Social Tragedies* (1900), the tragedy at this point being the decline of breast-feeding.

FROM The Poet's Prothalamion

"How could I cheat those lips of their true food?
Lo, here! God gave me these two sacred founts.
He gave me womanhood. Then shame on her
Who leaves to kine the task her God assigned.
She is but half a mother and full cheeks
And virgin bust bought with an empty heart
Are costly beauties. Father of my child
To be, my noble Lover, speak to me!
Tell me that motherhood is more to thee
Than virgin bloom! Or, if thy lips are mute,
Take what thine eyes are pleading and thy lips
But now and oft ere now have chastely begged!
Touch these white yoked lilies that still sleep!
Thou wilt find speech!" Thou saidst, and drewst aside
The drapery from thy bosom. My lips touched
Its faultless argent.

ELLA WHEELER WILCOX (1850–1919)

Communism

When my blood flows calm as a purling river,
  When my heart is asleep and my brain has sway,
It is then that I vow we must part for ever,
  That I will forget you, and put you away
Out of my life, as a dream is banished
  Out of the mind when the dreamer awakes;
That I know it will be when the spell has vanished,
  Better for both of our sakes.

When the court of the mind is ruled by Reason,
  I know it is wiser for us to part;
But Love is a spy who is plotting treason,
  In league with that warm, red rebel, the Heart.
They whisper to me that the King is cruel,
  That his reign is wicked, his law a sin,
And every word they utter is fuel
  To the flame that smoulders within.

And on nights like this, when my blood runs riot
  With the fever of youth and its mad desires,
When my brain in vain bids my heart be quiet,
  When my breast seems the centre of lava-fires,
Oh, then is the time when most I miss you,
  And I swear by the stars and my soul and say
That I will have you, and hold you, and kiss you,
  Though the whole world stands in the way.

And like Communists, as mad, as disloyal,
  My fierce emotions roam out of their lair;
They hate King Reason for being royal—
  They would fire his castle, and burn him there.

O Love! they would clasp you, and crush you, and
    kill you,
  In the insurrection of uncontrol.
Across the miles, does this wild war thrill you,
  That is raging in my soul?

ANONYMOUS (fl. mid-20th century)

The body of John Keats has not customarily been given British burial. However, as Timothy Hilton has observed (citing this in the *New Statesman* as his favorite bad marriage of poetry and politics), there seems small point in topographical fussiness.

FROM On Visiting the Graves of Keats and Marx in Hampstead Churchyard

John and Karl
Lying together
Under the earth
We need you now!

T. E. BROWN (1830–1897)

"Social Science"

O happy souls, that mingle with your kind,
    That laugh with laughers, weep with weepers,
Whom use gregarious to your like can bind,
    Who sow with sowers, reap with reapers!

To me it is not known,
The gentle art to moan
With moaners, wake with wakers, sleep with sleepers.

It must be good to think the common thought,
To learn with learners, teach with teachers;
To hold the adjusted soul till it is brought
To pray with prayers, preach with preachers.
But I can never catch
The dominant mode, nor match
The tone, and whine with whiners, screech with screechers.

Yet surely there is warmth, if we combine
And loaf with loafers, hunt with hunters;
It is a comfort as of nozzling swine
To row with rowers, punt with punters—
How is it then that I
Am alien to the style,
Nor ever swill with swillers, grunt with grunters?

I cannot choose but think it is a blessing
To fool with fools, to scheme with schemers;
To feel another's arms your soul caressing,
To sigh with sighers, dream with dreamers—
But I can't hit the span,
The regulation man,
Ephemer decent with his co-ephemers.

Yet, after all, if frustrate of this pleasure,
To eat with eaters, drink with drinkers,
If I can't find the Greatest Common Measure,
And cheat with cheaters, wink with winkers,
At any rate the struggle
My truer self to juggle,
And force my mind to fit
The standard ell of wit,

Shall never dwarf nor cramp me,
Shall never stint nor scamp me
So that I bleat with bleaters, slink with slinkers.

Thus spake I once, with fierce self-gratulation,
Nor hoped with hopers, feared with fearers;
Yet, discontent, it seemed a mere privation
To doubt with doubters, sneer with sneerers:
It seemed more happiness
A brother's hand to press,
To talk with talkers, hear with hearers.

Wherefore, albeit I know it is not great,
Mobbing with mobs, believing with believers,
Yet for the most it is a snugger state
To gain with gainers, grieve with grievers,
Than, desolate on a peak,
To whet one's lonely beak,
And watch the beaver huddling with the beavers.

But though this boon denied, my soul, love thou
The lover, gibe not with the giber!
O ragged soul! I cannot piece thee now
That, thread to thread, and fibre unto fibre,
Thou with another soul
Shouldst make a sentient whole:
But I am proud thou dost retain
Some tinct of that imperial *murex* grain
No carrack ever bore to Thames or Tiber.

ALFRED, LORD TENNYSON (1809–1892)

FROM Locksley Hall Sixty Years After

Authors—essayist, atheist, novelist, realist, rimester, play your part,

Paint the mortal shame of nature with the living
hues of art.

Rip your brothers' vices open, strip your own foul
passions bare;
Down with Reticence, down with Reverence—forward—naked—let them stare.

Feed the budding rose of boyhood with the drainage
of your sewer;
Send the drain into the fountain, lest the stream
should issue pure.

Set the maiden fancies wallowing in the troughs of
Zolaism—
Forward, forward, aye, and backward, downward too
into the abysm!

THOMAS HOOD (1799–1845)

Hood, one of the supreme masters of the pun in English, drove himself unmercifully, grinding out light verse intended to be funny. In this, probably his most popular poem, apparently he was serious.

The Bridge of Sighs

"Drown'd! drown'd!"—Hamlet

One more unfortunate,
Weary of breath,
Rashly importunate,
Gone to her death!

Take her up tenderly,
Lift her with care;
Fashion'd so slenderly,
Young, and so fair!

Look at her garments
Clinging like cerements;
Whilst the wave constantly
Drips from her clothing;
Take her up instantly,
Loving, not loathing.—

Touch her not scornfully;
Think of her mournfully,
Gently and humanly;
Not of the stains of her,
All that remains of her
Now is pure womanly.

Make no deep scrutiny
Into her mutiny
Rash and undutiful:
Past all dishonour,
Death has left on her
Only the beautiful.

Still, for all slips of hers,
One of Eve's family—
Wipe those poor lips of hers
Oozing so clammily.

Loop up her tresses
Escaped from the comb,
Her fair auburn tresses;
Whilst wonderment guesses
Where was her home?

Who was her father?
Who was her mother?
Had she a sister?
Had she a brother?
Or was there a dearer one
Still, and a nearer one
Yet, than all other?

Alas! for the rarity
Of Christian charity
Under the sun!
Oh! it was pitiful!
Near a whole city full,
Home she had none.

Sisterly, brotherly,
Fatherly, motherly
Feelings had changed:
Love, by harsh evidence,
Thrown from its eminence;
Even God's providence
Seeming estranged.

Where the lamps quiver
So far in the river,
With many a light
From window and casement,
From garret to basement,
She stood, with amazement,
Houseless by night.

The bleak wind of March
Made her tremble and shiver
But not the dark arch,
Or the black flowing river:
Mad from life's history,
Glad to death's mystery,

Swift to be hurl'd—
Any where, any where
Out of the world!

In she plunged boldly,
No matter how coldly
The rough river ran,—
Over the brink of it,
Picture it—think of it,
Dissolute Man!
Lave in it, drink of it,
Then, if you can!

Take her up tenderly,
Lift her with care;
Fashion'd so slenderly,
Young, and so fair!

Ere her limbs frigidly
Stiffen too rigidly,
Decently,—kindly,—
Smooth, and compose them
And her eyes, close them,
Staring so blindly!

Dreadfully staring
Thro' muddy impurity,
As when with the daring
Last look of despairing
Fix'd on futurity.

Perishing gloomily,
Spurr'd by contumely,
Cold inhumanity,
Burning insanity,
Into her rest.—
Cross her hands humbly

As if praying dumbly,
Over her breast!

Owning her weakness,
Her evil behaviour,
And leaving, with meekness,
Her sins to her Saviour!

MARTIN FARQUHAR TUPPER (1810–1889)

The Anglo-Saxon Race

A RHYME FOR ENGLISHMEN.

Stretch forth! stretch forth! from the south to the north!
From the east to the west,—stretch forth! stretch forth!
Strengthen thy stakes, and lengthen thy cords,—
The world is a tent for the world's true lords!
Break forth and spread over every place,
The world is a world for the Saxon Race!

England sowed the glorious seed,
In her wise old laws, and her pure old creed,
And her stout old heart, and her plain old tongue,
And her resolute energies, ever young,
And her free bold hand, and her frank fair face,
And her faith in the rule of the Saxon Race!

Feebly dwindling day by day,
All other races are fading away;
The sensual South, and the servile East,
And the tottering throne of the treacherous priest,

And every land is in evil case
But the wide scatter'd realm of the Saxon Race!

Englishmen everywhere! brethren all!
By one great name on your millions I call,—
Norman, American, Gael, and Celt,
Into this fine mixed mass ye melt,
And all the best of your best I trace
In the golden brass of the Saxon Race!

Englishmen everywhere! faithful and free!
Lords of the land, and kings of the sea,—
Anglo-Saxons! honest and true,
By hundreds of millions my word is to you,—
Love one another! as brothers embrace!
That the world may be blest in the Saxon Race!

ANONYMOUS (fl. 1857)

This memorable piece of protest poetry was rediscovered by Professor Richard Walser in an old issue of the Fayetteville *North Carolinian.*

Ode to a Ditch

RESPECTFULLY DEDICATED TO THE TOWN COMMISSIONERS

Oh, ditch of all ditches,
Death's store-house of riches,
Where wan disease slumbers mid festoons of slime!
Oh, dark foetid sewer,
Where death is the brewer
And *ail* is the liquor he brews all the time!

Oh, hot-bed of fever,
That fatal bereaver
Whose fiery breath blights the blossom of life!
Oh, palace of miasm
Whose hall is a chasm
Where pestilence revels and poison is rife!

Where, where on the earth,
From the place of Sol's birth
To the couch of his rest in the cloud-curtained West,
Is a ditch full as thou
Of the treasures which now
The phantom king hides in thy green oozy breast?

When Summer's sun beams,
What glorious steams
From Fever's foul kitchen, the sewer, will rise
Whose fragrance inhaled
Has never yet failed
Sending wicked men—somewhere—good men to the
skies.

What vapors will creep,
In the night when men sleep,
From thy cavernous recesses forth to the air;
And go on their mission
To feed the physician
And treat the dry graveyard to noggins of *bier!*

Oh, trench of all trenches!
Oh, stench of all stenches,
Far worse than the dead quails of Israel and Moses:
To look on thy slough
The Lord knows is enough,
But words can't express the emotions of noses!

Oh, wonderful sewer,
Each year brings a newer
And ghostlier charm to thy cavernous deeps!
More puppies and cats,
To say nothing of rats,
And offal and filth of all manner in heaps.

Mobilgas

IX

Philosophy

"Is life worth living?" Question that
Of old made wisest sages shiver . . .
—William Howard Mitchell,
"Acknowledging a Bouquet"

HENRY DAVID THOREAU (1817–1862)

"A true poem is not known by a felicitous expression, or by any thought it suggests, as much as by the fragrant atmosphere which surrounds it," Thoreau wrote in his journal in 1840. Emerson had apparently caught a strong whiff of some of Henry's early verses and advised him to burn them all. Thoreau followed this advice and regretted it later; nevertheless he did continue to produce and preserve poems which, if not actually putrescent, were not always possessed of the "air of Comeliness" prescribed in the *Journal*. Along with most readers, Thoreau was aware that his true forte was prose. In fact, he considered prose superior in general to poetry; he and the muse parted by mutual consent. "The poet often only makes an irruption, like a Parthian," he said, "and is off again, shooting while he retreats; but the prose writer has conquered like a Roman, and settled colonies." A parting shot follows.

My Boots

Anon with gaping fearlessness they quaff
The dewy nectar with a natural thirst,
Or wet their leathern lungs where cranberries lurk,
With sweeter wine than Chian, Lesbian, or Falernian
far.
Theirs was the inward lustre that bespeaks
An open sole—unknowing to exclude
The cheerful day—a worthier glory far
Than that which gilds the outmost rind with darkness
visible—
Virtues that fast abide through lapse of years,
Rather rubbed in than off.

WALT WHITMAN (1819–1892)

While it is easy to parody the good gray solitary singer, that strange uncommon man who sang *for*, if not exactly *with* the masses of mid-nineteenth century America, it is not equally easy to catch him nodding at the loom. Like Melville, much that appears crude or verbose in his poetry turns out on close inspection to make its own kind of poetic sense on one level or another, particularly if one connects poem to poem in his grand design. His work tends either to attract or repel, and very often this depends both on the basic temperament of the reader and what is in current fashion. Reading all the way through *Leaves of Grass* is a little like listening to Wagner's Ring cycle at one sitting; it is possible but not likely. Every year the New York radio station, WBAI, broadcasts the entire Ring to celebrate Washington's birthday. There should be a simultaneous reading of the *Leaves of Grass* to give a true melding of oversoul and that which lies underfoot.

FROM Thou Mother with Thy Equal Brood

Thou wonder world yet undefined, unform'd, neither
 do I define thee,
How can I pierce the impenetrable blank of the
 future?
I feel thy ominous greatness evil as well as good,
I watch thee advancing, absorbing the present, tran-
 scending the past,
I see thy light lighting, and thy shadow shadowing,
 as if the entire globe,
But I do not undertake to define thee, hardly to
 comprehend thee,

I but thee name, thee prophesy, as now,
I merely thee ejaculate!

THOMAS HOLLEY CHIVERS (1809–1858)

FROM Railroad Song

Clitta, clatta, clatta, clatter,
Like the devil beating batter
Down below in iron platter—
Which subsides into a clanky,
And a clinky, and a clanky,
And a clinky, clanky, clanky,
And a clanky, clinky, clanky;
And the song that I now offer
For Apollo's Golden Coffer—
With the friendship that I proffer—
Is for Riding on a Rail.

EDMUND VANCE COOKE (1866–1932)

The Rotarian glad-handedness of Edmund Vance Cooke, author of *Chronicles of the Little Tot* and *Impertinent Poems,* is never sunnier than on the way to the cemetery. Rarely with such good cheer has the conviction been expressed that whether one is dead or alive doesn't matter.

How Did You Die?

Did you tackle the trouble that came your way
   With a resolute heart and cheerful?

Or hide your face from the light of day
  With a craven soul and fearful?
Oh, a trouble's a ton, or a trouble's an ounce,
  Or a trouble is what you make it,
And it isn't the fact that you're hurt that counts,
  But only how did you take it?

You are beaten to earth? Well, well, what's that?
  Come up with a smiling face,
It's nothing against you to fall down flat,
  But to lie there—that's disgrace.
The harder you're thrown, why, the higher you
    bounce;
  Be proud of your blackened eye!
It isn't the fact that you're licked that counts;
  It's how did you fight—and why?

And though you be done to the death, what then?
  If you battled the best you could,
If you played your part in the world of men,
  Why, the Critic will call it good.
Death comes with a crawl, or comes with a pounce,
  And whether he's slow or spry,
It isn't the fact that you're dead that counts,
  But only how did you die?

T E. BROWN (1830–1897)

FROM Pain

The man that hath great griefs I pity not;
  'Tis something to be great
  In any wise, and hint the larger state,
Though but in shadow of a shade, God wot!

Moreover, while we wait the possible,
  This man has touched the fact,
  And probed till he has felt the core, where, packed
In pulpy folds, resides the ironic ill.

And while we others sip the obvious sweet—
  Lip-licking after-taste
  Of glutinous rind, lo! this man hath made haste,
And pressed the sting that holds the central seat.

For thus it is God stings us into life,
  Provoking actual souls
  From bodily systems, giving us the poles
That are His own, not merely balanced strife.

SYDNEY DOBELL (1824–1874)

From Dobell's Spasmodic tragedy, *Balder*, here is a scene in which the hero suffers a moment of inner crisis. Notable is the line in which Dobell counts out exactly ten *ah*'s, preserving the consistency of his pentameter.

FROM *Balder*, Scene XXXVIII

The Hill-side. Enter BALDER.

BALDER. Was this world built for happiness, that
    man
In all his agonies since pain began
Hath, as of intuition, changed its use
And customary order; made the Night
A banquet-hall for his cold feast of Death,
And Day his weary chamber? Or was't wrought
In equal seasons, that the separate walls

Of twain but neighbouring mansions might contain
The happy and the wretched?
I that walked
All this long night upon the bare hill-top
Grow heavy in the sunshine and would sleep.
[*He lies down and sleeps—after a while starts up.*]
This dream! why I came leaping out of it
Half-witted and half-dead as one escapes
From dungeons into air. I must have wept, too,
The grass below my face is all bedewed,—
Away!
[*Turns and sleeps—Leaps up with disordered looks.*]
No, no, it cannot be, it must not be,
It shall not be!—Amy!—
[*Looking up, his eye catches the clouds.*]
You white full heavens!
You crowded heavens that mine eyes left but now
Shining and void and azure!—
Ah! ah! ah!
Ah! ah! ah! ah! ah! ah! ah! ah! ah! ah!
By Satan! this is well. What! am I judged?
You ponderous and slow-moving minister's,
Are you already met? Are crimes begot
Above? And do we sin to give the train
And hungry following of the stately gods
An office? Doth their pastime tarry there
Because I lag? Is it to be endured
That while I sleep the ready forum forms
About me, and the conscript fathers wait
The unaccomplished wrong? Hence! clear the heavens!
Break up! What! can I not so much as dream
But your substantial thunders must surround
The ghostly fault, and with material towers
And bodily environment hem in
The thin unflesh'd commission? Do you close
Upon me like a weary prey run down,

Stalked to the final onset? But I live!
Will you sit at the board while the meal walks?
How if you are too soon? Who sees the game?
Look down upon us here—which is your man?
What have I done? My hands are white—behold!
Your solemn imperturbable o'er-high
All-seeing and prededicate avengers,
For once ye sit in vain! My will is not
Yours; nor shall any terrors of your loud
Discomfiture, nor any warning sign—
No, tho' the rocked right half of heaven rolled o'er
And stood at heaps on the sinister side—
Unplant my fixed resolve. Mine eyes do pierce
The lower ostentations of your brief
And temporary royalty to reach
A Paramount Supreme.

GRACE TREASONE (fl. 1963)

A column for local poets, "This Way to Parnassus" in the Morris County (New Jersey) *News*, first published this rare display of the metaphysical imagination still operating.

Life

Life is like a jagged tooth
that cuts into your heart;
fix the tooth and save the root,
and laughs, not tears, will start.

THOMAS HARDY (1840–1928)

FROM The Beauty

"The Regent Street beauty, Miss Verrey, the Swiss confectioner's daughter, whose personal attractions have been so mischievously exaggerated, died of fever on Monday evening, brought on by the annoyance she had been for some time subject to."

—London paper, October 1828.

O do not praise my beauty more
  In such world-wild degree,
And say I am one all eyes adore;
  For these things harass me!

. . . .

The inner I O care for, then,
  Yea, me and what I am,
And shall be at the gray hour when
  My cheek begins to clam.

EDGAR A. GUEST (1881–1959)

Guest, a native of Birmingham, England, once declared that he didn't think himself a poet at all—an opinion with which critics have agreed unanimously. For many years he provided the Detroit *Free Press* with a poem a day, including Sundays. Most of these 11,000-odd works celebrate raisin pie and other homely objects, or give clear-cut moral advice; but a deathless song lyric, "School Days," reveals an uncommon talent for alliteration. Guest's work was widely syndicated, collected and recollected (beginning with *A Heap o' Living* in 1916), read on the radio and embossed on greeting cards. A biography by Royce Holmes (1955) is must reading

FROM The Crucible of Life

Sacred and sweet is the joy that must come
From the furnace of life when you've poured off the
scum.

J. P. SARTRE

X

Science and Medicine

And when Life's prospects may at times appear dreary to ye,
Remember Alois Senefelder, the discoverer of lithography.

—William McGonagall,
"The Sprig of Moss"

Inoculation, heavenly maid, descend!

—An opening line,
cited by Coleridge,
Biographia Literaria

Sure *England* hath the Hemeroids, and these
On the North Posterne of the patient seize . . .

—John Cleveland,
"The Rebel Scot'

WILLIAM DIAPER (1685–1717)

Diaper, who placed among our nature poets for his submarine pastorals, went down to the sea again in 1722. With one John Jones, he published a complete Englishing of Oppian's *Halieuticks: Of the Nature of Fishes,* taken from the Greek and cast into heroic couplets. "Far from being a bridle, translation was to Diaper a spur to irrepressible excursions in figurative expression," observes Dorothy Broughton in her edition of Diaper's *Complete Works* (London, 1952). Diaper must have been carried away in the following passages from Book One, detailing certain fishes' habits of mating and reproduction.

FROM Oppian's *Halieuticks*

When pleasing Heat, and fragrant Blooms inspire
Soft leering Looks, kind Thoughts and gay Desire,
Love runs thro' All; the feather'd Wantons play,
Seek out their Mates, and bill on ev'ry Spray.
The savage Kinds a softer Rage express,
And gloating Eyes the secret Flame confess.
But none like Fishes feel the dear Disease;
For *Venus* doubly warms her native Seas.
Males unconcern'd their pleasing Loves repeat,
While anxious She's the ripen'd Birth compleat.
On sandy Mounds their pressing Bellies lay,
And force the Burden of the Womb away.
Close joyn'd the complicated Eggs remain;
To separate that Heap is racking Pain.
Complain no more, ye Fair, of partial Fate,
What Sorrows on the teeming Bride await.

The Female-Curse is not to Earth confin'd,
Severest Throws the Fishes Wombs unbind;
Lucina is alike to All unkind.
  Now when the vernal Breeze has purg'd the Air,
To ev'ry Shore the vig'rous Males repair;
By Fear compell'd, or Appetite inclin'd,
To chace the weak, or fly the stronger Kind:
Nor will the am'rous Females stay behind:
No Fears or Dangers can the Bliss prevent,
When urg'd by Love, and on the Joy intent,
They still importunate their Suit renew,
And obstinately kind extort their Due.
Their Bodies meet, the close Embraces please,
Till mingled Slime lies floating on the Seas:
The She's gulp greedy down the tepid Seed,
And fruitful from the strange Conception breed.
Hence the succeeding Colonies increase,
And new-spawn'd Tribes replenish all the Seas.
  But some no lawless Liberties allow;
Whose Brides confin'd their private Chambers know.
In close Retreat they guard th' imprison'd Fair,
Observe their Haunt, and watch with jealous Care,
Lest some false Leman should invade their Right,
And wanton glory in the stol'n Delight.
All Things obey, when softer Passions move,
But Fishes feel the keenest Rage of Love.

. . . .

  Strange the Formation of the *Eely* Race,
That know no Sex, yet love the close Embrace.
Their folded Lengths they round each other twine,
Twist am'rous Knots, and slimy Bodies joyn;
Till the close Strife brings off a frothy Juice,
The Seed that must the wriggling Kind produce.
Regardless They their future Offspring leave,
But porous Sands the spumy Drops receive.
That genial Bed impregnates all the Heap,

And little *Eelets* soon begin to creep.
Half-Fish, Half-Slime they try their doubtful strength,
And slowly trail along their wormy Length.
What great Effects from slender Causes flow!

RICHARD SAVAGE (1697–1743)

Most people who read Savage do so to figure out what Dr. Johnson saw in him. It is an open question. In the following lines, despite their subtitle, the poet seems less concerned for his patron the Duke's health than for the recent interesting discovery of little animals swimming about in semen, examined by microscope.

The Animalcule, A Tale

OCCASION'D BY HIS GRACE THE DUKE OF RUTLAND'S RECEIVING THE SMALL POX BY INOCULATION.

I

In *Animalcules*, Muse display
  Spirits, of Name unknown in Song!
Reader a kind Attention pay,
  Nor think an useful Comment long.

II

Far less than Mites, on Mites they prey;
  Minutest Things may Swarms contain:
When o'er your Iv'ry Teeth they stray,
  Then throb your little Nerves with Pain.

III

Fluids, in Drops, minutely swell;
  These subtil Beings Each contains;

In the small sanguine Globes they dwell,
  Roll from the Heart, and trace the Veins.

IV

Through ev'ry tender Tube they rove,
  In finer Spirits, strike the Brain;
Wind quick through ev'ry fibrous Grove,
  And seek, through Pores, the Heart again.

V

If they with purer Drops dilate,
  And lodge where Entity began,
They actuate with a genial Heat,
  And kindle into future *Man*.

VI

But, when our lives are Nature's Due,
  Air, Seas, nor Fire, their Frames dissolve;
They Matter, through all Forms, pursue,
  And oft to genial Heats revolve.

VII

Thus once an *Animalcule* prov'd,
  When *Man*, a Patron to the Bays;
This Patron was in *Greece* belov'd;
  Yet Fame was faithless to his Praise.

VIII

In *Rome*, this *Animalcule* grew,
  Mæcenas, whom the Classics rate!
Among the *Gauls*, it prov'd *Richlieu*,
  In Learning, Pow'r, and Bounty Great.

IX

In *Britain*, *Hallifax* it rose;
  (By *Hallifax*, bloom'd *Congreve*'s Strains)
And now it re-diminish'd glows,
  To glide through godlike *Rutland*'s Veins.

X

A Plague there is, too Many know;
  Too seldom perfect Cures befall it.
The *Muse* may term it *Beauty's Foe*;
  In *Physick*, the *Small Pox* we call it.

XI

From *Turks* we learn this Plague t'asswage,
  They, by admitting, turn its Course:
Their Kiss will tame the Tumor's Rage;
  By yielding, they o'ercome the Force.

XII

Thus *Rutland* did its Touch invite,
  While, watchful in the ambient Air,
This little, guardian, subtil Spright
  Did with the Poison *in* repair.

XIII

Th' Infection from the Heart it clears;
  Th' Infection, now dilated thin,
In pearly Pimples but appears,
  Expell'd upon the Surface Skin.

XIV

And now it, mould'ring, wastes away:
  'Tis gone!—doom'd to return no more!
Our *Animalcule* keeps its Stay,
  And must new Labyrinths explore.

XV

And now the *Noble's* Thoughts are seen,
  Unmark'd, it views his Heart's Desires!
It now reflects what It has been,
  And, rapt'rous, at its Change admires!

XVI

Its pristine Virtues, kept, combine,
  To be again in *Rutland* known;
But they, immers'd, no longer shine,
  Nor equal, nor encrease his own.

THOMAS CAREW (1594?–1640)

Thomas Carew, whose Muse Suckling described as "hard-bound," was a gentleman of the privy chamber. "While Carew held this office," we are told, "he displayed his tact and presence of mind by stumbling and extinguishing the candle he was holding to light Charles I into the queen's chamber, because he saw that Lord St. Albans had his arm round her majesty's neck. The king suspected nothing, and the queen heaped favours on the poet." He was later the king's taster.

Celia Bleeding, to the Surgeon

Fond man, that canst believe her blood
  Will from those purple channels flow;
Or that the pure untainted flood
  Can any foul distemper know;
Or that thy weak steel can incise
The crystal case wherein it lies:

Know, her quick blood, proud of his seat,
  Runs dancing through her azure veins;
Whose harmony no cold nor heat
  Disturbs, whose hue no tincture stains:
And the hard rock wherein it dwells
The keenest darts of love repels.

But thou repli'st, "Behold, she bleeds!"
  Fool! thou'rt deceiv'd, and dost not know
The mystic knot whence this proceeds,
  How lovers in each other grow:
Thou struck'st her arm, but 'twas my heart
Shed all the blood, felt all the smart.

WILLIAM WORDSWORTH (1770–1850)

"At Jedborough," Wordsworth explains, "my companion and I went into private lodgings for a few days; and the following Verses were called forth by the character and domestic situation of our Hostess." (The poem is part of *Memorials of a Tour in Scotland, 1803.*)

FROM The Matron of Jedborough and Her Husband

The more I looked, I wondered more,
And, while I scanned them o'er and o'er,
Some inward trouble suddenly
Broke from the Matron's strong black eye—
A remnant of uneasy light,
A flash of something over-bright!
Nor long this mystery did detain
My thoughts;—she told in pensive strain
That she had borne a heavy yoke,
Been stricken by a twofold stroke;
Ill health of body; and had pined
Beneath worse ailments of the mind.

JAMES WHITCOMB RILEY (1849–1916)

Most Americans encountering the James Whitcomb Riley stop on the Indiana Turnpike remember Riley (if at all) as the author of "The Ole Swimmin' Hole," "When the Frost Is on the Punkin," or "Little Orphan Annie" (not the comic strip). First honorary member of the American Academy of Arts and Letters and unquestionably the most popular American poet of his day, Riley used Hoosier dialect to celebrate homely love-objects. That millions responded would seem to prove the truth that (as Don Marquis once observed in a fictitious preface to the novels of Harold Bell Wright) it's moral worth gets the mazuma, and it can't be faked. In *Babbitt*, Sinclair Lewis has the newspaper poet Chum Frink moan into his cups that he'd had it in him to be another Riley, if he hadn't sold out.

Recently, at a college in Indiana, visiting engineers were obliged to sit through a critical and biographical lecture on Riley that (one engineer said) had opened worlds to him. Who knows but that somewhere south of the Gene Stratton Porter service plaza, *The Girl of the Limberlost*, too, may be yielding its precious metal in the afterglare of the New Criticism?

The Little Hunchback

I'm nine years old! an' you can't guess how much I
weigh, I bet!
Last birthday I weighed thirty-three! An' I weigh
thirty yet!
I'm awful little for my size—I'm purt' nigh littler 'an
Some babies is!—an' neighbors all calls me "The
Little Man!"
An' Doc one time he laughed and said: "I 'spect,
first thing you know,

You'll have a spike-tail coat an' travel with a show!"
An' nen I laughed—till I looked round an' Aunty
  was a-cryin'—
Sometimes she acts like that, 'cause I got "curv'ture
  of the spine!"

I set—while Aunty's washing—on my little long-leg
  stool,
An' watch the little boys and girls a-skippin' by to
  school;
An' I peck on the winder an' holler out an' say:
"Who wants to fight the little man 'at dares you
  all to-day?"
An' nen the boys climbs on the fence, an' little girls
  peeks through,
An' they all say: " 'Cause you're so big, you think
  we're 'feared o' you?"
An' nen they yell, and shake their fist at me, like I
  shake mine—
They're jist in fun, you know, 'cause I got "curv'ture
  of the spine!"

At evening, when the ironin's done, an' Aunty's
  fixed the fire,
An' filled an' lit the lamp, and trimmed the wick
  an' turned it higher,
An' fetched the wood all in fer night, an' locked the
  kitchen door,
An' stuffed the ole crack where the wind blows in
  up through the floor—
She sets the kittle on the coals, an' biles an' makes
  the tea,
An' fries the liver an' mush, an' cooks a egg fer me;
An' sometimes—when I cough so hard—her elder-
  berry wine
Don't go so bad fer little boys with "curv'ture of the
  spine."

But Aunty's all so childish like, on my account, you see,
I'm 'most feared she'll be took down—an' 'at's what bothers me—
'Cause ef my good ole Aunty ever would git sick an' die,
I don't know what she'd do in Heaven—till I come, by an' by,
For she's so ust to all my ways, an' everything, you know,
An' no one there like me, to nurse, an' worry over so—
'Cause all the little childrens there's so straight an' strong an' fine,
They's nary angel 'bout the place with "curv'ture of the spine."

JOHN DRYDEN (1631–1700)

The terrible effects of smallpox (and an overdose of Metaphysical ingenuity) urged Dryden to this very early effort.

FROM Upon the Death of the Lord Hastings

Blisters with pride swelled; which through's flesh did sprout
Like rose-buds, stuck i' th'lily-skin about.
Each little pimple had a tear in it,
To wail the fault its rising did commit . . .

ERASMUS DARWIN (1731–1802)

Darwin's *The Botanic Garden* is a long poem in two parts: *The Economy of Vegetation* and *The Loves of the Plants*, each of which takes—with its notes—an entire volume. The second part is a summary of the Linnean classification, with Rosicrucian machinery. The passage that follows is an explanation of a hybrid, supposedly a cross between a pink and a clove. Darwin may be a great poet, and it is not always possible to separate his heights from his depths.

FROM The Loves of the Plants

Caryo's sweet smile Dianthus proud admires,
And gazing burns with unallow'd desires;
With sighs and sorrows her compassion moves,
And wins the damsel to illicit loves.
The Monster-offspring heirs the father's pride,
Mask'd in the damask beauties of the bride.
So, when the Nightingale in eastern bowers
On quivering pinion woos the Queen of flowers;
Inhales her fragrance, as he hangs in air,
And melts with melody the blushing fair;
Half-rose, half-bird, a beauteous Monster springs,
Waves his thin leaves, and claps his glossy wings;
Long horrent thorns his mossy legs surround,
And tendril-talons root him to the ground;
Green films of rind his wrinkled neck o'erspread,
And crimson petals crest his curled head;
Soft warbling beaks in each bright blossom move,
And vocal Rosebuds thrill the enchanted grove!—
Admiring Evening stays her beamy star,
And still Night listens from his ebon car;
While on white wings descending Houries throng
And drink the floods of odour and of song.

XI

Art

Literary is a work very difficult to do.

—Julia A. Moore
from Preface to her collection,
A Few Choice Words to the Public
(1878)

JOHN KEATS (1795–1821)

In personality and character, Keats may well have been the first poet in English literary history to be entirely likable. Far from coinciding with Byron's notion of the frail will-o'-the-wisp, hypersensitive to criticism ("that fiery particle . . . snuffed out by an article"), Keats, when critics shot down *Endymion*, bravely went back to his drawing-board. Lately he has inspired several hefty biographies, that by Robert Giddings being of special interest for its appendices on Keats's use of the bawdy, and on whether the poet ever contracted venereal disease. In justice, we should note that Keats himself did not publish the following lines.

Lines on Seeing a Lock of Milton's Hair

Chief of organic numbers!
  Old Scholar of the Spheres!
Thy spirit never slumbers
  But rolls about our ears,
For ever, and for ever!
O what a mad endeavour
      Worketh he,
Who to thy sacred and ennobled hearse
Would offer a burnt sacrifice of verse
      And melody.

How heavenward thou soundest,
  Live Temple of sweet noise,
And Discord unconfoundest,
  Giving Delight new joys,
And Pleasure nobler pinions!

O, where are thy dominions?
Lend thine ear
To a young Delian oath,—aye, by thy soul,
By all that from thy mortal lips did roll,
And by the kernel of thine earthly love,
Beauty, in things on earth, and things above
I swear!

When every childish fashion
Has vanish'd from my rhyme,
Will I, grey-gone in passion,
Leave to an after-time,
Hymning and harmony
Of thee, and of thy works, and of thy life;
But vain is now the burning and the strife,
Pangs are in vain, until I grow high-rife
With old Philosophy,
And mad with glimpses of futurity!

For many years my offering must be hush'd;
When I do speak, I'll think upon this hour,
Because I feel my forehead hot and flush'd,
Even at the simplest vassal of thy power,—
A lock of thy bright hair,—
Sudden it came,
And I was startled, when I caught thy name
Coupled so unaware;
Yet, at the moment, temperate was my blood.
I thought I had beheld it from the flood.

LIZZIE DOTEN (1829–1890 or later)

Lizzie Doten, a "Spiritual trance-speaker," frequently did her stuff before large audiences. A facile versifier in her own right, she also tuned in on the posthumous works of Shakespeare, Burns, and Poe. Dictated from the hereafter, these were collected in *Poems from the Inner Life* (Boston, 1863), a volume which racked up at least eleven editions. Modestly, Miss Doten professed herself too weak a vessel to receive work of Shakespeare's usual caliber ("O World! somewhat I have to say to thee," one soliloquy begins). Burns, a pleasant master, beamed her a stronger signal; but Poe just about wrecked her. "Under his influence," she related, "I suffered the greatest exhaustion of vital energy: so much so, that after giving one of his poems, I was usually quite ill for several days." This extract comes from Poe's valediction to the world—uttered after Miss Doten (apparently) had had enough of him.

FROM Farewell to Earth

I would bear a love Platonic to the souls in earthly life;
I would give a sign Masonic to the heroes in the strife;
I have been their fellow-craftsman, bound apprentice to that Art,
Whereby Life, that cunning draughtsman, builds his temple in the heart.
But with Earth no longer mated, I have passed the First Degree;
I have been initiated to the second mystery.
O, its high and holy meaning not one soul shall fail to see!
Now, with loftiest aspirations, onward through the worlds I march,
Through the countless constellations, upward to the Royal Arch.
"Come up higher!" cry the angels: "come up to the Royal Arch."

SARAH TAYLOR SHATFORD (fl. 1916–1924)

As Lizzie Doten had done before her, Mrs. Shatford did her best to help the Bard of Avon overcome death and expand his bibliography. Off to a modest start with a book of her own verses (*Zekiel's Homespun Philosophies*, Boston, 1916), she then gave herself exclusively to transcribing new works by Shakespeare, who between 1919 and 1924 used her to divest himself of four hefty volumes. The first of these was *Shakespeare's Revelations*, "by Shakespeare's Spirit through the medium of his pen SARAH TAYLOR SHATFORD, Dictated exactly as herein found. No illiteracies, no obliterations, chargable to the Medium. My hand and seal hereon. W. S. In spirit." One of these Revelations follows.

Found

I who write here came here to find
An instrument for Shakespeare's mind.
To write my plays I did intend,
Their scurrility amend.
To take each line and blot for aye
The work for which I here shall pay
Before another plane shall see
My soul befouled, or I can be
Uplifted where my own went on
When life for them meant truly dawn!
To do this task then I must find
A mortal having spirits' mind.
Then must she be allotted me,
Before such harvest garnered be.

Through time I cannot count, or know,
I searched here, ay, high and low,

To learn where sat the instrument
Who could and would serve my intent.
Four years have passed since this one found
Her purposes while on the ground
Would be to answer when I spoke,
Nor any plea of mine revoke.
She knew me not while I knew her,
And all her life-pulse e'er could stir:
She wrote her poems writ by me,
Nor dreamed one there she could not see.
Till all was finished, books complete,
I claimed no throne but just a seat
Where daily spirit-food was spread
By Shakespeare, whom all men have read.
When in the end I spoke she heard,
As here she hears my every word—
And on to purpose great and high
We press, to prove men cannot die.

Her work was hers, as hers 'twill pass;
My work is mine, but mine, alas;
For any word that I may rhyme
Is but to prove no lust or crime
Can do for one, however great,
Naught when he comes to spirit-state.

Two thousand thousand eons sped
With SUCH recorded, is he DEAD:
And from the last his God shall give,
He mourns, through time, that he must live.

To gather naught but thistles, then,
He comes to warn his fellowmen
Lest they, as he, pass out, nor "die,"
But find themselves, as here am I.
Such will my work be then from now
Recorded by one, I allow,

Is more than just my stick (pencil) or pen,
—A saviour of her brothermen.
(Her task is hard which I have set;
But Shakespeare knows it will be met.)
W. S. In spirit (Through S.S.)

CYRIL R. MICHAEL (fl. 1941)

A diversified cast inhabits the verse of Cyril Michael, (*Come Back to Hindustan and Me and Other Poems*), from Hitler to Shirley Temple. Internal evidence suggests that Michael may have been a clerk in His Majesty's customs warehouse, writing under an extraordinarily British nom de plume. He reveals, at any rate, a decidedly chauvinistic and aeronautical turn of mind: his poems are dedicated to Sir Thomas Alexander, governor of Bihari ("whose gentle influence and attractive personality," claims Michael, "did much to assist me on my inspired flight"), and all profits from their sale go to the Royal Air Force.

Shirley Temple

When all the world was sore depressed,
And sadness held its thrall,
And each one to themselves confessed,
This is the end of all!
This sordid hemisphere is dull,
No happiness is here,
When thro' the gloom, and thro' the lull,
There came a voice of cheer!

For Shirley Temple made her bow,
And sang her songs renown,

And from that time, till this day now,
Mankind have lost their frown.
Her lilt has made children rejoice,
Old men to shed a tear,
Heart-broken mothers found their choice,
And hugged their mem'ries dear.

Shirley, unconscious of her art,
Gave forth a wealth of song,
And took her great allotted part,
To help the world along.
Thus everybody wears a smile,
The universe is changed,
Gone is the once disgruntled style,
All things are rearranged.

WALT WHITMAN (1819–1892)

Trickle Drops

Trickle drops! my blue veins leaving!
O drops of me! trickle, slow drops,
Candid from me falling, drip, bleeding drops,
From wounds made to free you whence you were prison'd,
From my face, from my forehead and lips,
From my breast, from within where I was conceal'd, press forth red drops, confession drops,
Stain every page, stain every song I sing, every word I say, bloody drops,
Let them know your scarlet heat, let them glisten,
Saturate them with yourself all ashamed and wet,
Glow upon all I have written or shall write, bleeding drops,
Let it all be seen in your light, blushing drops.

ADELAIDE ANN PROCTER (1825–1864)

Miss Procter, who usually concealed herself under the pseudonym Mary Berwick, was in part responsible for Sir Arthur Sullivan's Song "The Lost Chord"—at one time the original for many a bawdy parody. Charles Dickens, particularly taken with her mind and character, wrote in an introduction to a volume of her fragile and often didactic verse, "No claim can be set up for her, thank God, to the possession of any of the conventional poetical qualities." If at times one half suspects that a tiny tigress lurks beneath Miss Procter's violets, it is too timid ever to show its claws and teeth for public inspection.

My Picture

Stand this way—more near the window—
  By my desk—you see the light
Falling on my picture better—
  Thus I see it while I write!

Who the head may be I know not,
  But it has a student air;
With a look half sad, half stately,
  Grave sweet eyes and flowing hair.

Little care I who the painter,
  How obscure a name he bore;
Nor, when some have named Velasquez,
  Did I value it the more.

As it is, I would not give it
  For the rarest piece of art;
It has dwelt with me, and listened
  To the secrets of my heart.

Many a time, when to my garret,
  Weary, I returned at night,
It has seemed to look a welcome
  That has made my poor room bright.

Many a time, when ill and sleepless,
  I have watched the quivering gleam
Of my lamp upon that picture,
  Till it faded in my dream.

When dark days have come, and friendship
  Worthless seemed, and life in vain,
That bright friendly smile has sent me
  Boldly to my task again.

Sometimes when hard need has pressed me
  To bow down where I despise,
I have read stern words of counsel
  In those sad, reproachful eyes.

Nothing that my brain imagined,
  Or my weary hand has wrought,
But it watched the dim Idea
  Spring forth into armèd Thought.

It has smiled on my successes,
  Raised me when my hopes were low,
And by turns has looked upon me
  With all the loving eyes I know.

Do you wonder that my picture
  Has become so like a friend?—
It has seen my life's beginnings,
  It shall stay and cheer the end!

JULIA A. MOORE (1847–1920)

The Author's Early Life

I will write a sketch of my early life,
  It will be of childhood day,
And all who chance to read it,
  No criticism, pray.
My childhood days were happy,
  And it fills my heart with woe,
To muse o'er the days that have passed by
  And the scenes of long ago.

In the days of my early childhood,
  Kent county was quite wild,
Especially the towns I lived in
  When I was a little child.
I will not speak of my birthplace,
  For if you will only look
O'er the little poem, My Childhood Days,
  That is in this little book.

I am not ashamed of my birthright,
  Though it was of poor estate,
Many a poor person in our land
  Has risen to be great.
My parents were poor, I know, kind friends,
  But that is no disgrace;
They were honorable and respected
  Throughout my native place.

My mother was an invalid,
  And was for many a year,
And I being the eldest daughter
  Her life I had to cheer.

I had two little sisters,
  And a brother which made three,
And dear mother being sickly,
  Their care it fell on me.

My parents moved to Algoma
  Near twenty-three years ago,
And bought one hundred acres of land,
  That's a good sized farm you know.
It was then a wilderness,
  With tall forest trees around,
And it was four miles from a village,
  Or any other town.

And it was two miles from a schoolhouse,
  That's the distance I had to go,
And how many times I traveled
  Through summer suns and winter snow.
How well do I remember
  Going to school many a morn,
Both in summer and in winter,
  Through many a heavy storm.

My heart was gay and happy,
  This was ever in my mind,
There is better times a coming,
  And I hope some day to find
Myself capable of composing.
  It was my heart's delight,
To compose on a sentimental subject
  If it came in my mind just right.

If I went to school half the time,
  It was all that I could do;
It seems very strange to me sometimes,
  And it may seem strange to you.
It was natural for me to compose,
  And put words into rhyme,

And the success of my first work
  Is this little song book of mine.

My childhood days have passed and gone,
  And it fills my heart with pain
To think that youth will nevermore
  Return to me again.
And now kind friends, what I have wrote,
  I hope you will pass o'er,
And not criticise as some have done,
  Hitherto herebefore.

THOMAS HARDY (1840–1928)

FROM The Abbey Mason

—When longer yet dank death had wormed
The brain wherein the style had germed

From Gloucester church it flew afar—
The style called Perpendicular.—

To Winton and to Westminster
It ranged, and grew still beautifuller . . .

JOHN CLEVELAND (1613–1658)

FROM The Rebel Scot

Ring the bells backward; I am all on fire.
Not all the buckets in a country choir

Shall quench my rage. A poet should be feared
When angry, like a comet's flaming beard.

ELIZABETH BARRETT BROWNING (1806–1861)

Mrs. Browning is unfairly represented here by part of "A Vision of Poets," a narrative in tercets about a bard afflicted with insomnia. Bemused in the woods, he meets a beautiful lady on a palfrey, who accosts him, "What ho, sir poet!"; and bids him drink from four mysterious pools, successively more disgusting. The poem goes on to reward the obliging drinker with face-to-face interviews with Homer, Hesiod, Ossian, Lope de Vega, Schiller, Cowley, Burns, Shelley, Keats, Coleridge, "poor, proud Byron, sad as grave, / And salt as life; forlornly brave, / And quivering with the dart he drave"; and others.

FROM A Vision of Poets

A fiery throb in every star,
Those burning arteries that are
The conduits of God's life afar.

A wild brown moorland underneath,
And four pools breaking up the heath
With white low gleamings blank as death.

Beside the first pool, near the wood,
A dead tree in set horror stood,
Peeled and disjointed, stark as rood;

Since thunder-stricken years ago,
Fixed in the spectral strain and throe
Wherewith it struggled from the blow:

A monumental tree, alone,
That will not bend in storms, nor groan,
But break off sudden like a stone.

Its lifeless shadow lies oblique
Upon the pool where, javelin-like,
The star-rays quiver while they strike.

"Drink," said the lady, very still:
"Be holy and cold." He did her will,
And drank the starry water chill.

The next pool they came near unto
Was bare of trees; there, only grew
Straight flags, and lilies just a few,

Which sullen on the water sate,
And leant their faces on the flat,
As weary of the starlight-state.

"Drink," said the lady, grave and slow:
"*World's use* behooveth thee to know."
He drank the bitter wave below.

The third pool, girt with thorny bushes,
And flaunting weeds and reeds and rushes
That winds sang through in mournful gushes,

Was whitely smeared in many a round
By a slow slime: the starlight swound
Over the ghastly light it found.

"Drink," said the lady sad and slow:
"*World's love* behooveth thee to know."
He looked to her commanding so;

Her brow was troubled; but her eye
Struck clear to his soul. For all reply
He drank the water suddenly,

Then, with a deathly sickness, passed
Beside the fourth pool and the last,
Where weights of shadow were downcast

From yew and alder, and rank trails
Of nightshade clasping the trunkscales,
And flung across the intervals

From yew to yew: who dares to stoop
Where those dank branches overdroop,
Into his heart the chill strikes up,

He hears a silent gliding coil,
The snakes strain hard against the soil,
His foot slips in their slimy oil,

And toads seem crawling on his hand,
And clinging bats, but dimly scanned,
Full in his face their wings expand.

A paleness took the poet's cheek:
"Must I drink *here*?" he seemed to seek
The lady's will with utterance meek:

"Ay, ay," she said, "it so must be:"
(And this time she spake cheerfully)
"Behooves thee know *world's cruelty*."

He bowed his forehead till his mouth
Curved in the wave, and drank unloath
As if from rivers of the south;

His lips sobbed through the water rank,
His heart paused in him while he drank,
His brain beat heart-like, rose and sank,

And he swooned backward to a dream
Wherein he lay 'twixt gloom and gleam.
With death and life at each extreme:

And spiritual thunders, born of soul,
Not cloud, did leap from mystic pole,
And o'er him roll and counter-roll,

Crushing their echoes reboant
With their own wheels. Did Heaven so grant
His spirit a sign of covenant?

At last came silence. A slow kiss
Did crown his forehead after this;
His eyelids flew back for the bliss.

The lady stood beside his head.
Smiling a thought with hair dispread:
The moonshine seemed dishevellèd . . .

SYDNEY DOBELL (1824–1874)

It seems appropriate at this point to recall a Spasmodic poet's libation to Mrs. Browning.

To the Authoress of "Aurora Leigh"

Were Shakespeare born a twin, his lunar twin
(Not of the golden but the silver bow)
Should be like thee: so, with such eyes and brow,

Sweeten his looks, so, with her dear sex in
His voice, (a king's words writ out by the queen)
Unman his bearded English, and, with flow
Of breastful robes about her female snow,
Present the lordly brother. Oh Last-of-kin,
There be ambitious Women here on earth
Who will not thank thee to have sung so well!
Apollo and Diana are one birth,
Pollux and Helen break a single shell.
Who may now hope? While Adam was alone
Eve was to come. She came; God's work was done.

XII

Faith and Morals

Our Saviour meek and with untroubled mind
After his airy jaunt . . .

—J. Milton,
Paradise Regained

ANONYMOUS (fl. 1754)

That the grimmer elements of the metaphysical tradition were slow to die out of English religious verse is apparent in this hymn from the middle of the eighteenth century. The present editors received it from William Cole, who got it from William Styron, who got it from Tom Ingram and Douglas Newton's *Hymns as Poetry* (London, 1956), which got it from *A Collection of Hymns of the Children of God in all Ages*, published by the Moravian Brethren.

FROM 'We greet each other in the Side'

We greet each other in the Side
  Of our beloved Spouse,
Which is ordained for his dear Bride
  Her everlasting House.
The Lamb, the Husband of our Hearts,
Hath got, 'tis true, more wounded Parts,
Yet is the bleeding lovely Side
The Chamber of the Bride.

Our Husband's Side-wound is indeed
  The Queen of all his Wounds;
On this the little Pidgeons feed,
  Whom Cross's Air surrounds.
There they fly in and out and sing,
Side's blood is seen on ev'ry wing,
The bill that picks the Side-hole's floor,
Is red of Blood all o'er.

. . . .

A bird that dives into the Side,
  Goes down quite to the Ground,

And finds a Bottom large and wide
  In this so lovely Wound.
A Side-hole's diver I will be:
O Side-hole! I will sink in thee.
My Soul and Body, enter thou
Into the *Pleura* now.

To live and work and sleep therein,
  I'm heartily inclin'd:
As a poor Dove myself to screen,
  Is my whole heart and mind.
O precious Side-hole's cavity!
I want to spend my Life in thee.
Glory to thee for thy Side-hole,
Dear Husband of my Soul!

With all my heart I bow and bend
  Before thy bleeding Feet:
Yet to thy Side I re-ascend,
  Which is to me most sweet.
There in one Side-hole's Joy divine,
I'll spend all future Days of mine.
Yes, yes, I will forever sit
There, where thy Side was split.

WILLIAM B. TAPPAN (fl. 1845)

It would seem churlish to mock the modest pieties and fervent praises of water-drinking apparent in Tappan's collection *Poetry of the Heart* (Worcester, Massachusetts, 1845). Many of his poems display an almost McGonagall-like fondness for catastrophes: especially shipwrecks, Papist plots, and conflagrations in orphan asylums.

FROM Song of the Three Hundred Thousand Drunkards in the United States.

We come! we come! to fill our graves,
  On which shall shine no star;
To glut the worm that never dies—
  Hurrah! hurrah! hurrah!

BRET HARTE (1836–1902)

This poem by Harte was set to music by Charles Gounod.

The Mission Bells of Monterey

O bells that rang, O bells that sang
Above the martyrs' wilderness,
Till from that reddened coast-line sprang
The Gospel seed to cheer and bless,
What are your garnered sheaves to-day?
O Mission bells! Eleison bells!
O Mission bells of Monterey!

O bells that crash, O bells that clash
Above the chimney-crowded plain,
On wall and tower your voices dash,
But never with the old refrain;
In mart and temple gone astray!
Ye dangle bells! Ye jangle bells!
Ye wrangle bells of Monterey!

O bells that die, so far, so nigh,
Come back once more across the sea;

Not with the zealot's furious cry,
Not with the creed's austerity;
Come with His love alone to stay,
O Mission bells! Eleison bells!
O Mission bells of Monterey!

M. KRISHNAMURTI (b. 1912)

The Cloth of Gold is a mystical dance-drama by a poet who exhibits what one critic called (according to the blurb) "pure genius, unimpeded." The snippet here comes at the very climax of the plot, whose intricacies must remain unintelligible to an audience not familiar with the *Mahabharata.*

FROM The Cloth of Gold

Now the last step! Behold,
He sees the Cloth of Gold—
The Mother's robe!—enfold

His wife! His wife no more!
No more, oh nevermore!
(The hellhounds rage and roar!)

The Rana bends his brow
And kneels . . . *My Mother thou!*
Were these the words that now

Broke from his lips? Oh doom!
O fateful doom! (Yea, boom
That dreaded word of gloom!)

The Spirit's Odyssey

I saw her first in gleams,
As one might see in dreams
    A moonmaiden undrape
    Her opalescent shape
Midst moveless lunar streams!

Now fierce and sudden-truth'd,
She smites me, sabre-tooth'd:
    As sunlight, snarling, crawls
    Into the bower and mauls
The waker, slumber-sooth'd!

ANONYMOUS (fl. 1845)

On Christmas eve, 1845, the engineer and the stoker of the Norwich-to-London train, perhaps inspired by holiday cheer, let out their throttle to see how fast the old crate would go. According to one eye-witness, they hit 60. These metaphysical lines come from their tombstone in Ely Cathedral.

'The Line to heaven by Christ was made'

The Line to heaven by Christ was made
With heavenly truth the Rails are laid,
From Earth to Heaven the Line extends
To Life Eternal where it ends.
Repentance is the Station then
Where Passengers are taken in,
No Fee for them is there to pay.
For Jesus is himself the way.

God's Word is the first Engineer
It points the way to Heaven so dear,
Through tunnels dark and dreary here
It does the way to Glory steer.
God's Love the Fire, his Truth the Steam,
Which drives the Engine and the Train,
All you who would to Glory ride,
Must come to Christ, in him abide
In First and Second, and Third Class,
Repentance, Faith and Holiness,
You must the way to Glory gain
Or you with Christ will not remain.
Come then poor Sinners, now's the time
At any Station on the Line.
If you'll repent and turn from sin
The Train will stop and take you in.

HENRY WADSWORTH LONGFELLOW
(1807–1882)

The work of Longfellow—a highly literate if low-keyed man who nearly always had his wits about him—disappoints the searcher of the execrable. Besides the immortal "Excelsior!" however, one must admire the following anecdote, in which a bright jiggetty-jog rhythm keeps leap-frogging over the back of abject piety.

FROM The Norman Baron

In his chamber, weak and dying,
Was the Norman baron lying;
Loud, without, the tempest thundered,
  And the castle-turret shook.

In this fight was Death the gainer,
Spite of vassal and retainer,
And the lands his sires had plundered,
  Written in the Doomsday Book.

By his bed a monk was seated,
Who in humble voice repeated
Many a prayer and pater-noster,
  From the missal on his knee;

And, amid the tempest pealing,
Sounds of bells came faintly stealing,
Bells, that from the neighboring kloster
Rang for the Nativity.

In the hall, the serf and vassal
Held, that night, their Christmas wassail;
Many a carol, old and saintly,
  Sang the minstrels and the waits;

And so loud these Saxon gleemen
Sang to slaves the songs of freemen,
That the storm was heard but faintly,
  Knocking at the castle-gates.

FRANCIS THOMPSON (1859–1907)

Thompson failed at nearly everything except poetry. Discharged from the army for incompetence, he earned a slim living for a while as a holder of horses' heads; but when finally too seedy in appearance to be let into the British Museum, had the good fortune to be picked up by a prostitute, and later to be befriended by Wilfred and Alice Meynell. Under the Meynells' care and shelter, he wrote some of his most ecstatic poems, shot through with a sort of rosy lambency.

Little Jesus

Ex ore infantium, Deus, et lactentium
perfecisti laudem

Little Jesus, wast Thou shy
Once, and just so small as I?
And what did it feel like to be
Out of Heaven, and just like me?
Didst Thou sometimes think of *there,*
And ask where all the angels were?
I should think that I would cry
For my house all made of sky;
I would look about the air,
And wonder where my angels were;

And at waking 'twould distress me—
Not an angel there to dress me!
Hadst Thou ever any toys,
Like us little girls and boys?
And didst Thou play in Heaven with all
The angels that were not too tall,
With stars for marbles? Did the things
Play *Can you see me?* through their wings?
And did Thy Mother let Thee spoil
They robes, with playing on *our* soil?
How nice to have them always new
In Heaven, because 't was quite clean blue!

Didst Thou kneel at night to pray,
And didst Thou join Thy hands, this way?
And did they tire sometimes, being young,
And make the prayer seem very long?
And dost Thou like it best, that we
Should join our hands to pray to Thee?
I used to think, before I knew,
The prayer not said unless we do.

And did Thy Mother at the night
Kiss Thee, and fold the clothes in right?
And didst Thou feel quite good in bed,
Kissed, and sweet, and Thy prayers said?

Thou canst not have forgotten all
That it feels like to be small:
And Thou know'st I cannot pray
To Thee in my father's way—
When Thou wast so little, say,
Couldst Thou talk Thy Father's way?—
So, a little Child, come down
And hear a child's tongue like Thy own;
Take me by the hand and walk,
And listen to my baby-talk.
To Thy Father show my prayer
(He will look, Thou art so fair),
And say: "O Father, I, Thy Son,
Bring the prayer of a little one."

And He will smile, that children's tongue
Has not changed since Thou wast young!

ANONYMOUS (fl. before 1965)

This ballad of undetermined origin, was circulated in a pass-around at the Dover (New Jersey) Senior Citizens Club.

Grass on the Prayer Path

From the converts in Uganda
Comes to us a story grander,
In the lesson that it teaches,
Than a sermon often preaches.

For they tell what sore temptations
Come to them; what need of patience,
And a need, all else outweighing,
Of a place for private praying.

So each convert chose a corner
Far away from eye of scorner,
In the jungle where he could
Pray to God in solitude.

And so often went he thither,
That the grass would fade and wither
Where he trod and you could trace
By the paths, each prayer place.

If they hear the evil tiding
That a brother is backsliding,
And that some are even saying,
"He no longer cares for praying,"

Then they say to one another,
Very soft and gently, "Brother,
You'll forgive us now for showing,
On your path the grass is growing."

And the erring one, relenting,
Soon is bitterly repenting:
"And how sad I am at knowing
On my path the grass is growing.

"But it shall be so no longer!
Prayer I need to make me stronger!
On my path so oft I'm going,
Soon no grass will there be growing."

Have a trysting place with God!
And keep a little path open!

JOHN BYROM (1692–1763)

Byrom made his reputation early, with a pastoral, "Colin and Phebe," published in the *Spectator* in 1714:

> My fair one is gone, and my joys are all drown'd;
> And my heart, I am sure, weighs more than a pound.

From then on, with some time out for preaching his sermons and for inventing a "Universal English Shorthand," he versified most of the events of his time and much of the theology of William Law. Sir Leslie Stephen, in his *History of English Thought in the Eighteenth Century*, attributes to Byrom "an almost morbid faculty of rhyming," though at his best, it might be noted, he was a good poet. Robert Duncan has paid the homage of quoting from Byrom in "Poem Beginning With a Line by Pindar."

FROM On Trinity Sunday

The one Divinity of Father, Son,
And Spirit, teaches Christian thought to shun
Both Pagan and Rabbinical mistake,
And understand what holy prophets spake,
Or in the ancient writings or the new,
To which this doctrine is the sacred clue,
That so conducts us to the saving plan
Of true religion, as no other can.

For were the Son's Divinity denied,
The Father's must of course be set aside,
Or be a dark one—How can it be bright,
But by its own eternal, inborn light?
The glory of the Father is the Son,
Of all his pow'rs begotten, or begun,
From all eternity—Take Son away,
And what the Father can delight in, say.

The love, paternally divine, implies
Its proper object, whence it must arise,
That is, the Son; and so the filial, too,
Implies paternal origin in view;
And hence the third distinctly glorious tie
Of love, which both are animated by:
All is One God, but He contains divine,
Living relations, evidently *Trine*.

CHARLIE D. TILLMAN (fl. 1890s)

Tillman was a hymn writer who operated his own publishing house in Atlanta, Georgia. In addition to his widely used hymn books ("These songs go," said Sam Jones of *The Revival No. 2*, "and they carry the people with them"), he published—and probably wrote—"Papa's Late Train," "Diamonds in the Rough," "Who Cares for Father," "Wandering Girl," "Mamma Kissed Me In a Dream," "Only a Brakeman," "Bettie and the Baby (with four other beautiful songs)," "Remember the Orphans," and "Little Empty Shoes My Baby Used to Wear." The words which follow are to the tune of "After the Ball."

Lost After All

1. A little child is kneeling by his mother's chair,
Softly repeating sweet words of prayer
"Dear Loving Jesus, Gentle and Mild
Look down, and bless me, thy little child."
Long kneels the Mother, praying that night,
"God bless my treasure, guide him a-right"
List to his story, weep o'er his fall,
Through his own madness, lost after all.

Refrain.

After the days of childhood;
After a Mother's prayer,
After the years of manhood,
Freighted with joys and cares;
After a thousand chances,
After the final call,
Bitter the wail of a spirit;
Lost after all.

2. Changed is the picture, years have swiftly flown,
Sadly the mother waits all alone.
Waits for her darling where does he roam,
Has he forgotten mother and home?
Hark, there's a footstep, surely, 'tis he.
Oh Heaven help her what does she see?
Inside he staggers, one groan, a fall;
Wrecked by the wine cup, lost after all.

3. Farther and farther from his Mother's God,
Wanders he on in sin's road so broad,
Till by the window one stormy night,
He finds her waiting lifeless and white:
Vainly the spirit strives for his soul,
Spurning his God he turns to the bowl.
Angels in Heaven, weep o'er his fall,
Still unrepentant, lost after all.

RICHARD CRASHAW (1612–1649)

Crashaw, one of the greatest of English poets, is not universally admired. For every devotee of his garlands of rich conceits, there is someone holding "The Weeper" at arm's length, laughing at Mary Magdalen's tears:

Two walking baths; two weeping motions;
Portable, & compendious oceans.

It is, says Austin Warren, "a poem so confectionary that we almost forget that these are tears and mistake them for *bonbons*." "The fourth stanza," Mario Praz adds mysteriously, "contains an unbearable pun." (These are the poet's admirers.) Crashaw, it seems, was one of those sublime fools who become wise through persisting in their folly. Only at times, as in these two epigrams, is his folly unredeemable.

Acts 8: On the baptized Ethiopian

Let it no longer be a forlorn hope
  To wash an Ethiop:
He's washt! his gloomy skin a peaceful shade
  For his white soul is made:
And now, I doubt not, the Eternal Dove
  A black-faced house will love.

Luke 11: Blessed be the paps which Thou hast sucked

Suppose he had been Tabled at thy Teats,
  Thy hunger feels not what he eats:
He'll have his Teat ere long (a bloody one).
  The Mother then must suck the Son.

ROBERT BROWNING (1812–1889)

Browning one day browsed among the Royalist rhymes and noted a scurrilous couplet on Sir Harry Vane:

'Tis said they will give him a cardinal's hat:
They sooner will give him an old nun's twat.

That last word struck him, he later told Dr. Furnivall, "as a distinctive part of a nun's attire that might fitly pair off with the cowl appropriated to a monk." (Dr. Furnivall's reaction is not recorded.) This led to the passage in *Pippa Passes* which Eric Partridge refers to as Browning's "hair-raising misapprehension,—the literary world's worst 'brick.' " (Pippa is speaking.)

FROM *Pippa Passes*

Oh, what a drear dark close to my poor day!
How could that red sun drop in that black cloud?
Ah, Pippa, morning's rule is moved away,
Dispensed with, never more to be allowed!
Day's turn is over, now arrives the night's.
O lark, be day's apostle
To mavis, merle, and throstle,
Bid them their betters jostle
From day and its delights!
But at night, brother owlet, over the woods,
Toll the world to thy chantry;
Sing to the bats' sleek sisterhoods
Full complines with gallantry:
Then, owls and bats,
Cowls and twats,
Monks and nuns, in a cloister's moods,
Adjourn to the oak-stump pantry!

XIII

Crime and Punishment

That letter sealed the young defendant's fate.
"He's got to be convicted!" cried the State.
"Ye gods!" he chuckled, "lazy luck, but great!"
—Harry Edward Mills,
"Convicted"

A crime it is, therefore in bliss
you may not hope to dwell;
But unto you I shall allow
the easiest room in Hell.
—Michael Wigglesworth,
"The Day of Doom," 1662
(God addressing the unbaptised infants)

FREDERICK FANNING AYER (1851–1924)

Like his fellow poet Wallace Stevens, Frederick Fanning Ayer conducted a public career as lawyer and (later) business executive while surreptitiously tilling his inner garden. Born in Lowell, Massachusetts, he took his B.A. from Harvard in 1873 and after the death of his father in 1878 succeeded to managing the properties of his family estate: among them, the J. C. Ayer Company, makers of patent medicines, and the Tremont & Suffolk Mills. Ayer served both companies as president. No piker, he presented the town of Ayer, Massachusetts, with an Ayer Memorial Library; and probably subsidized publication in 1911 of one mammoth collection of his poems, *Bell and Wing* (1,266 pages, weight three pounds, eleven ounces). A lifelong bachelor, Ayer bent his energies to the theme of thwarted love; and resembled Browning in his convoluted syntax and his fondness for the dramatic monologue (usually spoken by a hideous gnome, a priest, or an acolyte). "Moon Fields, or Man the God," a 102-page work of Miltonic science-fiction, mostly in couplets, shows Ayer's knotty individualism in its very first lines:

> My moon, not yours, nor any triune—
> God-lorded or Paul-Petered moon . . .

"The Indictment," here given in somewhat abbreviated form, enables him to bubble and seethe with bitterest execrations.

FROM The Indictment

I

Down underground,
So too overhead,

I've the teeth of a hound,
  I've the blue of the dead
And the cold as well,
  I've the humor of Hell
To cudgel and slay,
  I've the dog in me
Of deformity,
  The dog and to have his day.

III

Up to the peak
  Of ugly thought
I glutton my freak,
  I daub my blot
Of blood in the cheek
  Of her girleen grace—
So runs the streak
  Down her handsome face—
In under the hair
  The eyes are there
At their glassen stare—

IV

So runs the cripple,
  The demon in me,
Shoulders put triple,
  Put niggardly,
As, lo, by nowl
  To the breast is bent
Just as my soul
  Is pinched and pent,
Pity as thin
  As the spider's heart
And his poison fin
  And his butcher's art.

V

My rival he,
  Mastrous straight
As majesty
  And smoothe as plate,
Polish to new
  His lively look,
Hair under glue,
  Collar to cook
So the end in view
  Be the end of you
In a match of pleats
  And ribbon feats.

VI

He has his day
  Of love with her,
And I must delay,
  I must not stir,
But watch him take
  His cup of bliss,
Behold him slake
  His thirst and kiss
Her mouth and eyes
  And pigeonwise
His love display
  Each day to day
To make her his prize
  His champion way.

VII

The cripple I,
  By way of birth,
Of my quarried eye,
  Of my crooked girth,
I could never say
  "I love you too,

I've the dimple-play,
  Apollo-thew,
I've the iris guise,
  So give me your eyes
Fo my picture-book
  And my hungry look"—
For so I should see
  My look in there
Of the hungry stare
  Of deformity.

IX

There stands the Law
  Which made me so
Of porbeagle jaw,
  Quohog toe:
I get the thing
  From broods of men
In the years before
  All reckoning;
Spring-time then
  Of a world to grow,
A beginning when
  Men thought to go
This way askew,
  That way awry,
To crush what is true,
  To hate what is high.

X

So only sent
  Their soul askew
From prosperment,
  From trueness, too;
Cultured what look
  The pit-viper has,

Took his oily crook,
  His nasty mass,
And just by the Law
  Of progeny
Handed their cloven claw
  To me,
Handed their spilth
  Of villainy,
Vileness and filth
  To me.

XI

This is the cellar-pit,
  This where she died,
I here to tell of it,
  Tell how I lied
By my trashy note,
  Tell how I tried
My thumbs in her throat:
  If I may not have her,
So shall not he
  By his puff-palaver,
His eaglery,
  His elegant pate
Of Roman speech,
  All out of reach
Of my muzzled gait.

XII

My thumbs in her throat,
  My teeth in her face,
How I tore and I smote
  The blood from its place
On the pillow of thought,
  Her thought of him
In his lucky lot,
  In his fawnish limb—

Her teeth I sowed
  In the cellar air
Till the dark pit glowed,
  Mocked at her stare,
Fingered and toed
  In her blood and hair—

XIII

"Take that," said I,
  "Take that and that,
Learn you to die
  As the hounded rat,
Learn you that I
  Am the hornèd bat
To stifle, to kill,
  To full fulfill
The beast in me,
  My savagery,
My dragon spell,
  Learn you to see
The fire in me
  Of all blazing Hell!"

XVII

And the pith of it all
  That I am so small
As the soul in you
  From which I grew
To a cloven claw
  Just to ripen for
Murder by beast of heart
  To hate, to play my part
Of vulture, crocodile art—
  And this her grave
In the cellar air,
  I the plain knave
To put her there
  For my devil's whim

And my withered limb—
  And I so small
Because you were so small,
  And, oh, the pity of it all!

WILLIAM WORDSWORTH (1770–1850)

As time went on, Wordsworth turned from recollecting lakes in tranquillity to meditating on capital punishment in high unease.

FROM Sonnets upon the Punishment of Death

VI

Ye brood of Conscience—Spectres! that frequent
The bad man's restless walk, and haunt his bed—
Fiends in your aspect, yet beneficent
In act, as hovering Angels when they spread
Their wings to guard the unconscious Innocent—
Slow be the Statutes of the land to share
A laxity that could not but impair
Your power to punish crime, and so prevent.
And ye, Beliefs! coiled serpent-like about
The adage on all tongues, "Murder will out,"
How shall your ancient warnings work for good
In the full might they hitherto have shown,
If for deliberate shedder of man's blood,
Survive not Judgment that requires his own?

CHARLOTTE BRONTË (1816–1855)

Life in the family parsonage in Haworth, Yorkshire, it seems, was enough to drive the Brontë sisters into a world of wild imaginings. Though critics lately have tended to regard Emily as the fairest blossom of the three, it was Charlotte's *Jane Eyre* that played the loudest tune on bookshop cash registers. Evidently she could turn on her Gothic thunder-and-lightning in meter, as well as in prose.

FROM Mementos

. . . And heaven did curse—they found him laid,
   When crime for wrath was ripe,
Cold—with the suicidal blade
   Clutched in his desperate gripe.

'Twas near that long-deserted hut,
   Which in the wood decays,
Death's axe, self-wielded, struck his root,
   And lopped his desperate days.

WILL CARLETON (1845–1912)

The fame of Will Carleton, once poet laureate of Michigan, is still commemorated by law in the Wolverine State: each year Will Carleton Day is set aside for the reading of his poems in Michigan public schools. Author of the justly famous "Over the Hill to the Poorhouse" and its sequel, "Over the Hill from the Poorhouse," Carleton published *Farm Ballads, Farm Legends, Farm Festivals* and other similar volumes in rapid succession. In a rare *ars poetica* he remarked that, "There is no thought so great, so complicated, so ineffably sublime, that it cannot be resolved into elements easily understood by the average human intellect." Eugene F. Gray, editor of one collection of Carleton's poems (in its twenty-fifth edition in 1927), remarked with sober admiration that "Carleton's readers experience rapid changes of emotions. The tears are nearly always followed by a hearty laughter."

FROM Johnny Rich

Raise the light a little, Jim,
For it's getting rather dim,
And, with such a storm a-howlin', 'twill not do to douse the glim.
Hustle down the curtains, Lu;
Poke the fire a little, Su;
This is somethin' of a flurry, mother, somethin' of a—whew!

Goodness gracious, how it pours!
How it beats ag'in the doors!
You will have a hard one, Jimmy, when you go to do the chores!
Do not overfeed the gray;
Give a plenty to the bay;
And be careful with your lantern when you go among the hay.

See the horses have a bed
When you've got 'em fairly fed;
Feed the cows that's in the stable, and the sheep that's in the shed;
Give the spotted cow some meal,
Where the brindle can not steal;
For she's greedy as a porker, and as slipp'ry as an eel.

Hang your lantern by the ring,
On a nail, or on a string;
For the Durham calf'll bunt it, if there's any such a thing:

He's a handsome one to see,
And a knowin' one is he:
I stooped over t'other morning, and he up and went
for me!

Rover thinks he hears a noise!
Just keep still a minute, boys;
Nellie, hold your tongue a second, and be silent with
your toys.
Stop that barkin', now, you whelp,
Or I'll kick you till you yelp!
Yes, I hear it; 'tis somebody that's callin' out for help.

WILLIAM McGONAGALL (1830–1902)

FROM Richard Pigott, the Forger

For by forged letters he tried to accuse Parnell
For the Phoenix Park murders, but mark what befell.
When his conscience smote him he confessed to the
fraud,
And the thought thereof no doubt drove him mad.

Then he fled from London without delay,
Knowing he wouldn't be safe there night nor day,
And embarked on board a ship bound for Spain,
Thinking he would escape detection there, but 'twas
all in vain.

Because while staying at a hotel in Spain
He appeared to the landlord to be a little insane.
And he noticed he was always seemingly in dread,
Like a person that had committed a murder and
afterwards fled.
And when arrested in the hotel he seemed very cool,
Just like an innocent schoolboy going to school.

And he said to the detectives, "Wait until my portmanteau I've got."
And while going for his portmanteau, himself he shot.

So perished Richard Pigott, a forger bold,
Who tried to swear Parnell's life away for the sake of gold,
But the vengeance of God overtook him,
And Parnell's life has been saved, which I consider no sin.

HARRY EDWARD MILLS (fl. 1901)

FROM Convicted

Around his open grave from near and far
Stood many former comrades of the bar,
Who mourned the brilliance of his earlier star.

The Judge unsealed his dying words and read:
"Dear friends; since I am numbered with the dead
Believe I beg you what herein is said.

"I did not kill the farmer, and I lied
When I confessed his tragic homicide.
May God forgive me, I was sorely tried."

They could not read the rest, for every word
By trickling blood had been forever blurred;
The truth they craved could only be inferred.

And so the Judge above the shrouded bier,
Reviewed the brilliant yet ill-starred career
Of him whose grief was fatally sincere.

XIV

Death

I have wandered home but newly
From this ultimate dim Thule.
—E. A. Poe,
"Dream-Land"

PERCY BYSSHE SHELLEY (1792–1822)

Shelley, even before exhorting the Irish peasants to revolution and the bishops of England to atheism, had written two Gothic novels. The second of these, *St. Irvyne; or the Rosicrucian,* contains the ballad of Sister Rosa from which an excerpt is given here. The mature vision of Shelley begins with *Alastor; or the Spirit of Solitude,* an allegory of the poetic quest:

> At length upon the lone Chorasmian shore
> He paused, a wide and melancholy waste
> Of putrid marshes.

But Mary Shelley, in the preface to her edition of his *Poetical Works,* provides the clearest statement of Shelley's idealistic aims: "To defecate life of its misery and its evil was the ruling passion of his soul."

FROM *St. Irvyne*

XIII

And the storm-fiends wild rave
O'er the new-made grave,
And dread shadows linger around.
The Monk called on God his soul to save,
And, in horror, sank on the ground.

XIV

Then despair nerved his arm
To dispel the charm,
And he burst Rosa's coffin asunder.
And the fierce storm did swell
More terrific and fell,
And louder pealed the thunder.

XV

And laughed, in joy, the fiendish throng,
  Mixed with ghosts of the mouldering dead:
And their grisly wings, as they floated along,
  Whistled in murmurs dread.

XVI

And her skeleton form the dead Nun reared
  Which dripped with the chill dew of hell.
In her half-eaten eyeballs two pale flames appeared,
And triumphant their gleam on the dark Monk
    glared,
  As he stood within the cell.

XVII

And her lank hand lay on his shuddering brain;
  But each power was nerved by fear.—
'I never henceforth, may breathe again;
Death now ends mine anguished pain.—
  The grave yawns,—we meet there.'

XVIII

And her skeleton lungs did utter the sound,
  So deadly, so lone, and so fell,
That in long vibrations shuddered the ground;
And as the stern notes floated around,
  A deep groan was answered from hell.

HENRY KIRKE WHITE (1785–1806)

While still in his teens, Kirke White crashed a literary society and talked on "Genius" for two and three-quarter hours solid. The society voted him their thanks. He was much admired by Robert Southey, who wrote a biography of him; another memoir assures us his "merits were unalloyed by a single vice." He died of tuberculosis.

On the Death of Dermody, the Poet

Child of Misfortune! Offspring of the Muse!
  Mark like the meteor's gleam his mad career;
    With hollow cheeks and haggard eye,
    Behold he shrieking passes by:
      I see, I see him near:
    That hollow scream, that deepening groan;
      It rings upon mine ear.

Oh come, ye thoughtless, ye deluded youth,
  Who clasp the siren pleasure to your breast,
    Behold the wreck of genius here,
    And drop, oh drop the silent tear
      For Dermody at rest:
    His fate is yours, then from your loins
      Tear quick the silken vest.

Saw'st thou his dying bed! Saw'st thou his eye,
  Once flashing fire, despair's dim tear distil;
    How ghastly did it seem;
    And then his dying scream:
      O God! I hear it still:
    It sounds upon my fainting sense,
      It strikes with deathly chill.

Say, didst thou mark the brilliant poet's death;
  Saw'st thou an anxious father by his bed,
    Or pitying friends around him stand:
    Or didst thou see a mother's hand
      Support his languid head?
    Oh none of these—no friend o'er him
      The balm of pity shed.

Now come around, ye flippant sons of wealth,
Sarcastic smile on genius fallen low;
Now come around who pant for fame,
And learn from hence, a poet's name
Is purchased but by woe:
And when ambition prompts to rise,
Oh think of him below.

For me, poor moralizer, I will run,
Dejected, to some solitary state:
The muse has set her seal on me,
She set her seal on Dermody,
It is the seal of fate:
In some lone spot my bones may lie,
Secure from human hate.

Yet ere I go I'll drop one silent tear,
Where lies unwept the poet's fallen head:
May peace her banners o'er him wave;
For me in my deserted grave
No friend a tear shall shed:
Yet may the lily and the rose
Bloom on my grassy bed.

ALPHEUS BUTLER (fl. 1929–1942)

One wonders at the fate of Alpheus Butler, whatever it may be. Stunning reviews greeted his *Make Way for Happiness* (Boston, 1932), in which appeared work from such journals and anthologies as *The Chicago Girl, Florida Poets: 1931, The Kynewisbok, The 1929 Grub Street Book of Verse,* and *One for Posterity.* Butler was last heard from in 1942, when he co-edited a *Book of Father Verse* (Minneapolis).

Death of a Fair Girl

Tall and fair
Was Sarah White
A buxom beauty
Gay and bright.

Her smiles intrigued
Several men
Aspiring to
Get in her ken.

Fair and tall
In her youth
Haughtily
She disdained truth.

But lived within
Days of jazz
When saxophones
Did not razz.

No calm, sweet hymns
For Sarah White.
Religion seemed
Dead and trite.

Deeper music
Of the soul
Was tabooed for
A gayer role.

Evenings never
Found her in.
Staid convention
Seemed a. sin

Sarah White
At twenty-eight
Is dead.
One wonders at her fate.

THEO. MARZIALS (fl. 1873)

This Victorian gem was recovered from oblivion by Christopher Adams for his exquisite anthology *The Worst English Poets* (London, 1958). It first appeared in a collection entitled *A Gallery of Pigeons*.

A Tragedy

Death!
Plop.
The barges down in the river flop.
Flop, plop,
Above, beneath.
From the slimy branches the grey drips drop,
As they scraggle black on the thin grey sky,
Where the black cloud rack-hackles drizzle and fly
To the oozy waters that lounge and flop
On the black scrag-piles, where the loose cords plop,
As the raw wind whines in the thin tree-top.
Plop, plop.
And scudding by
The boatmen call out hoy! and hey!
And all is running in water and sky,
And my head shrieks—"Stop,"
And my heart shrieks—"Die."

My thought is running out of my head;
My love is running out or my heart;

My soul runs after, and leaves me as dead,
For my life runs after to catch them—and fled
They are all every one!—and I stand, and start,
At the water that oozes up, plop and plop,
On the barges that flop
                    And dizzy me dead.
I might reel and drop.
                            Plop
                            Dead.
And the shrill wind whines in the thin tree-top.
    Flop, plop.

A curse on him.
                    Ugh! yet I knew—I knew—
If a woman is false can a friend be true?
It was only a lie from beginning to end—
  My Devil—my "Friend"
I had trusted the whole of my living to!
  Ugh! and I knew!
      Ugh!
  So what do I care,
And my head is as empty as air—
      I can do,
      I can dare
    (Plop, plop,
    The barges flop
    Drip, drop.)
      I can dare, I can dare!
And let myself all run away with my head,
And stop.
      Drop
      Dead.
    Flip, flop.
      Plop.

THOMAS HOLLEY CHIVERS (1807–1858)

Chivers accused Poe of plagiarizing "The Raven" from his own "To Allegra Florence in Heaven." It was, to quote Professor Damon again, "the end of Chivers's literary reputation. This Humpty-Dumpty conceit has bid fair to outlive all his other works. Critics had but to quote his own defense, and his case was laughed out of court."

FROM To Allegra Florence in Heaven

As an egg, when broken, never
Can be mended, but must ever
Be the same crushed egg forever—
  So shall this dark heart of mine!
Which, though broken, is still breaking,
And shall nevermore cease aching
For the sleep which has no waking—
  For the sleep which now is thine!

LYDIA H. SIGOURNEY (1791–1865)

Mrs. Sigourney, of Hartford, Connecticut, published no fewer than fifty books. Known as "the American Hemans," she wrote an elegy when the real Felicia Hemans died, in which all nature is represented as mourning for the author of "The boy stood on the burning deck . . ."

FROM On the Death of Mrs. Felicia Hemans

The little plant that never sang before,
Save one sad requiem, when its blossoms fell,

Sighs deeply through its drooping leaves for thee,
As for a florist fallen.

TOMBSTONE EPITAPHS

When in centuries gone by most British and American tombstones were decorated with verses, every village churchyard offered its own anthology. Here are a few specimens, reasonably well authenticated.

Moulton, Cambridgeshire:

Sacred to the memory
of Lettuce Manning
Oh, cruel death
  To satisfy thy palate,
Cut down our Lettuce
  To make a salad.

Elton, Dorsetshire:

Robert Roch and John Antrem, 1669
The bodys here of two divines embrace,
Both which were once the Pastors of this place:
And if their corps each other seem to greet,
What will they do when soul and body meet?

Winstead, Connecticut:

Aaron S. Burbank, 1818–1883
Bury me not when I am dead
Lay me not down in a dusty bed

I could not bear the life down there
With earth worms creeping through my hair.

Pelham, Massachusetts:

Warren Gibbs, Died by arsenic
poisoning Mar. 23, 1860,
Aged 36 yrs., 5 ms., 23 dys.

Think my friends when this you see
How my wife has done for me
She in some oysters did prepare
Some poison for my lot and fare
Then of the same I did partake
And Nature yielded to its fate.
Before she my wife became
Mary Felton was her name.
Erected by his brother Wm. Gibbs

Jersey, Channel Islands (on a brewer):

Here lies poor Burton,
He was both hale and stout;
Death laid him on his bitter bier,
Now in another world he hops about.

New Bern, North Carolina:

Ingenuous youth, thou art laid in dust,
Yet Joseph Moodey s name continue must.

Providence, Rhode Island:

Hear Lyes Sidney Snyder
1803–1823
The wedding day decided was,
The wedding wine provided
But ere the day did come along
He drunk it up and died, did.
Ah, Sidney! Sidney!

Pewsey, Wiltshire:

Here lies the body
of
Lady O'Looney
commonly called the Sublime
She was
Bland, passionate and deeply religious
Also she painted
In water colors,
And sent several pictures
To the exhibition.
She was the first cousin
To Lady Jones
And of such
Is the kingdom of Heaven.

JOHN DANFORTH (1660–1730)

John Danforth was a Massachusetts divine and, as the standard study puts it, "the least famous member of the Danforth clan of poets." He wrote mostly epitaphs and elegies, including "A Funeral Poem in

Memory of Mr. Hopestill Clap" and "A Pindarick Elegy Upon the Renowned Mr. Samuel Willard" where he frankly admits

> His Virtue's Roll's so large, Th'Ocean's so Deep;
> My Verse could do no more, but only creep
> And Spy, and Speak a little on the Brink.

Danforth is said to have been a learned man. For some reason or other, he was buried in the tomb of Lieutenant Governor Stoughton.

FROM Pindarick Elegy Upon the Renowned Mr. Samuel Willard

In Crimson Flood, wave Thousands to his Tomb,
Swell'd Big with Heroe's Blood, like Trojane
  Womb:
Troy were forgot,
But for our Parallel Lott;
Ah! Woful Day! One Conquering Horse of Fate
Severe & Just, Enter'd our Opened Gate;
Nay 'Twas a Troop,
Enough to Seize, and swallow up
Long horded Stores that made Us Rich, & Proud,
That many Scores of Plenteous years had bounteously
  bestow'd.
Such Losing Bankrupts We; 'Twould break
  Heaven too
But that it's Wealth is Infinite, to Set us up Anew.

EMILY DICKINSON (1830–1886)

'A Dying Tiger—Moaned for Drink'

A Dying Tiger—moaned for Drink—
I hunted all the Sand—

I caught the Dripping of a Rock
And bore it in my Hand—

His Mighty Balls—in death were thick—
But searching—I could see
A Vision on the Retina
Of Water—and of me—

'Twas not my blame—who sped too slow—
'Twas not his blame—who died
While I was reaching him—
But 'twas—the fact that He was dead—

ALI S. HILMI TÖREL (fl. 1953)

Nirvana

Few broken coughs . . . Then blood, a sobbing sigh!
Result of love unheard, unseen, untold!
Another cough and sobs . . . There laid, behold!
A girl in bed about to say good-bye.
Her dad concealing tears: "You'll live, not die!"
Cried she: "Don't let night fall! I'm growing cold!
Oh, God, I'm coming fast. No fears—I'm bold!"
The after day all prayed: "In peace there lie!"
She left the world and all for good behind,
And chose at heart in paradise to dwell
With him who'd gone before—for her to wait.
On Earth, in paradise they both were kind,
And each to other suited fine and well.
Nirvana was their lovely happy gait!

ALFRED, LORD TENNYSON (1809–1892)

Claribel

A MELODY

Where Claribel low-lieth
  The breezes pause and die,
    Letting the rose-leaves fall;
But the solemn oak-tree sigheth,
    Thick-leaved, ambrosial,
  With an ancient melody
  Of an inward agony,
Where Claribel low-lieth.

At eve the beetle boometh
  Athwart the thicket lone;
At noon the wild bee hummeth
  About the moss'd headstone;
At midnight the moon cometh,
  And looketh down alone.
Her song the lintwhite swelleth,
The clear-voiced mavis dwelleth,
  The callow throstle lispeth,
The slumbrous wave outwelleth,
  The babbling runnel crispeth,
The hollow grot replieth
  Where Claribel low-lieth.

JULIA A. MOORE (1847–1920)

Little Libbie

One more little spirit to Heaven has flown,
To dwell in that mansion above,
Where dear little angels, together roam,
In God's everlasting love.

One little flower has withered and died,
A bud near ready to bloom,
Its life on earth is marked with pride;
Oh, sad it should die so soon.

Sweet little Libbie, that precious flower
Was a pride in her parents' home,
They miss their little girl *every* hour,
Those friends that are left to mourn.

Her sweet silvery voice no more is heard
In the home where she once roamed;
Her place is *vacant* around the hearth,
Where her friends are mourning lone.

They are mourning the loss of a little girl,
With black eyes and auburn hair,
She was a treasure to them in this world,
This beautiful child so fair.

One morning in April, a short time ago,
Libbie was active and gay;
Her Saviour called her, she had to go,
Ere the close of that pleasant day.

While eating dinner, this dear little child
Was choked on a piece of beef.

Doctors came, tried their skill awhile,
  But none could give relief.

She was ten years of age, I am told,
  And in school stood very high.
Her little form now the earth enfolds,
  In her embrace it must ever lie.

Her friends and schoolmates will not forget
  Little Libbie that is no more;
She is waiting on the shining step,
  To welcome home friends once more.

MATTIE J. PETERSON (1866–1947)

The Poetissima Laureatissima of Bladen County, North Carolina, has attracted fierce partisans, who claim for her a supremacy over the Sweet Singer of Michigan. Miss Peterson's case rests upon a single volume: *Little Pansy, A Novel, and Miscellaneous Poetry* (Wilmington, North Carolina, 1890), in which occurs this piece, with its celebrated metrical description of her father's walk. Other passages combine a rare mawkishness with the greatest syntactical complexity:

There about many persimmon trees,
  Of which in the past was made beer,
And it was enjoyed much by me,
  Which becomes as a fountain clear.

For the facts of her life all are in debt to Richard Walser of North Carolina State University, who has edited the Poetissima's book in facsimile (Charlotte, North Carolina, 1967). Sentenced to a career of schoolteaching by a childhood affliction that had left her too weakly to marry a farmer, Miss Peterson sought comfort in literature. Her novel, a gumdrop of Gothic sentiment, is noted for (among other things) its hero's marriage proposal: "I love Jesus above all, and you next." On hearing (through a lonely hearts club) from a Texan willing to order her by mail sight unseen, Miss Peterson shut down her schoolroom, hastily packed, and lit out of town at two in the morning. She seems to have written no more after that; and died at age 81 in Hillsboro, Texas, having belted down half a large watermelon.

I Kissed Pa Twice After His Death

I kissed dear Pa at the grave,
  Then soon he was buried away;
Wreaths were put on his tomb,
  Whose beauty soon decay.

I lay down and slept after the burial:—
  I had started to school I dreamed,
But had left my books at home,
  Pa brought them it seemed.

I saw him coming stepping high,
  Which was of his walk the way;
I had stopped at a house near by—
  His face was pale as clay.

When he lay under a white sheet
  On the morning after his decease,
I kissed his sad and sunken cheek,
  And hoped his spirit had found peace.

When he was having convulsions
  He feared he would hurt me;

Therefore told me to go away.
  He had dug artichokes for me.

Pa dug the artichokes on that day,
  He never will dig any more;
He has only paid the debt we owe.
  We should try to reach the shining shore.

INDEX

Page numbers for authors of poems included in this anthology are indicated by **boldface.**